Guarding the Gospel

Biblical Faith and the Future of United Methodism

By James V. Heidinger II

Guarding the Gospel
Biblical Faith and the Future of United Methodism
Copyright ©2007 Forum for Scriptural Christianity, Inc.

Art direction, cover, and layout: Robert Rempfer
Editor: Steve Beard
Assistant editor: Krista Hershey

First printed by Living Streams Publications, March 2007

Living Streams Publications is a ministry of Good News, a renewal movement within the United Methodist Church.

For more information, contact:
Good News
308 East Main Street
P.O. Box 150
Wilmore, KY 40390

(859) 858-4661

This book is dedicated to the following
faithful servants and colleagues in renewal:

William N. Henderson
Virginia Law Shell
Edmund W. Robb Jr.
William H. Hinson
Diane L. Knippers
Robert D. Snyder
David A. Seamands

Contents

Part 4 - Faithfulness in Oversight

INTRODUCTION

This generation has witnessed the rise of what have come to be known as renewal movements or ministries within the historic mainline/oldline denominations in America. This year, 2007, Good News will celebrate its 40th Anniversary of ministry! We are one of the oldest of such ministries, seeking to help bring doctrinal and spiritual renewal and ecclesial reform to the United Methodist Church.

Every mainline denomination in North America has experienced the emergence of renewal ministries, as each has been infected by the same virus. The feverish symptoms in these various communions are quite similar: membership loss, lack of spiritual vitality, loss of the authority of Scripture, decline of world mission, doctrinal confusion and revisionism, pro-homosexual activism, and the embracing of trendy, fad theologies.

These conditions are neither new nor recent for United Methodism. I was ordained an elder in the East Ohio Annual Conference in 1969. For more than 35 years, the revisionist themes have changed very little. They go something like this: The Scriptures are of human origin, not divine; Jesus was not born of a virgin, nor was He raised from the dead; Jesus never really claimed divinity for himself and was, therefore, no different than you or me; Jesus didn't ascend into heaven, and thus will not be coming again; and, humankind is basically good, not sinful, and all that is needed is education and the opportunity for our inherent goodness to blossom. I have heard these themes across the years from some of our United Methodist pastors and theologians, have read them in our publications, and have spoken with distraught church members whose pastors have preached these themes from their pulpits.

It is difficult for laity to comprehend just why a United Methodist pastor or theologian would invest a lifetime in Christian ministry if the doctrines and teachings of one's church were not true. This problem has a long history, dating back to the early 1900s, when theological liberalism had a major impact on all of the mainline denominations in the United States. As the intellectual currents of the New Science and Social Darwinism swept across the nation, they challenged the supernatural foundations of the Christian faith. Churches were unprepared for the onslaught of this new thought.

It was in this intellectual milieu that theological Liberalism emerged as a movement which tried to accommodate the Christian faith to the new rational, secular, and anti-supernatural axioms that were fast finding a home in America. Theological liberalism was, essentially, an attempt to make the gospel more acceptable to "modern man."

Simply put, liberalism tried to excise the supernatural elements out of the biblical text. The historicity of the gospels was replaced with a vague admiration of Jesus as a good teacher, but not the risen Lord. Liberalism's main thrust was to focus on the moral and ethical teachings of Jesus, urging folks to do their best to follow his example in the face of urgent social problems facing the nation at the time.

This new teaching in the American church resulted in the tragic loss of the transcendent dimension of the gospel, of divine revelation, and confidence in God's power to transform individual lives. This led to an increasingly vacuous new theology, characterized by a loss of the sense of the broken relationship between God and man. H. Richard Niebuhr described this new theology with his oft-cited, devastating critique: "A God without wrath brought men without sin into a kingdom without judgment through ministrations of a Christian without a cross" (*The Kingdom of God in America*, 1956).

During this period, Rudolph Bultmann, a German New Testament scholar, would gain a huge following in American theological education. In the midst of this rational, secular milieu, he would insist that "virtually nothing reliable could be known about Jesus." He rejected the virgin birth and the resurrection, among other things, as primitive nonsense. If the faith were to be meaningful to modern men and women, Bultmann insisted that Christians must stop trying to defend the historicity of Christianity (which he believed could not stand up to scientific scrutiny), and instead take refuge in feelings and personal experience.

Many of these very sentiments have carried on into the present generation, as illustrated by the much-publicized, highly controversial Jesus Seminar. This self-selected group of scholars meets periodically to discuss, debate, and cast votes on what they think Jesus actually said and did (using color-coded cards to vote). Many of us agree with Candler School of Theology's Luke Timothy Johnson that the selection of the seminar members was based not on quality of scholarship but on prior agreement to discover a particular "Jesus." That is, a Jesus who fits the "countercultural attitude favored by liberal academics." Johnson believes their bias generates "bad history and bad theology."

It is in this theological milieu that Good News has carried on its renewal ministry for 40 years. It is in the context of these continuing theological concerns, and issues related to them, that Good News is publishing this volume of my essays that have appeared in GOOD NEWS magazine in recent years.

If I have a life verse, it is II Timothy 1:14, in which Paul urges young Timothy, "Guard the good deposit that was entrusted to you—guard it with the help of the Holy Spirit who lives in us." The idea Paul is expressing is for Timothy to guard this "good deposit," the message of the gospel, to make sure it not be damaged, lost, or distorted. The fact is that even in the early days of the church there were those who wanted to change, corrupt and distort the message of the gospel. Timothy was to be on the watch and so must we today.

For those of us who have been ordained as United Methodist elders, we promised several things when a bishop laid hands upon us. Publicly, we promised that we would "faithfully proclaim the Word of God, and defend the church against all doctrine contrary to the Word of God." I confess a bit of impatience with pastors who feel no personal responsibility for challenging erroneous, revisionist teachings that are being offered today in lieu of the truth of the gospel. It's as if a new commandment has been given us, to go into all the United Methodist world and spread tranquility.

I have heard some of my United Methodist colleagues admit they are weary of the battle for the truth of the gospel. I understand what they are saying. I have been involved with these matters here at Good News for more than 25 years now. Some even see it as a distraction from the real ministry of the church. But Presbyterian renewalist, the Rev. Sue Cyre, has it right when she insists that these battles are not a *distraction* from real ministry: "The battle over truth and falsehood *is* the real ministry of the church. Everywhere the church goes, it is to proclaim the truth of the gospel but it is always against a backdrop of some false beliefs." Sue goes on to quote John Calvin, who, in speaking of the long-term nature of spiritual warfare, said, "Peace is not the norm, the battle is."

So, at the heart of the essays in this volume are matters of serious theological concern. And as I have compiled this volume, I have been reminded of numerous colleagues in renewal who have served faithfully and engaged the church on matters of biblical truth. A number of these colleagues have in recent years "finished the course" and become a part of the Church Triumphant. They are friends and leaders whom we deeply miss. It is to seven of these friends and colleagues that this book is dedicated.

Dr. William N. Henderson was my father in the faith and in the ministry. He introduced me during my teenage years to a vital, life-transforming gospel during his pastorate in Fairfield, Illinois in the late 1950s. At least five of us young people entered full-time Christian service as a result of Bill's five-year ministry in Fairfield. I will be eternally grateful for Bill's life and fruitful ministry. Throughout his lifetime, he was involved in, and supportive of, most all of the United Methodist renewal ministries. He died in 1999.

Mrs. Virginia Law Shell was a Life-time Honorary Board Member of Good News and for seven years a columnist for GOOD NEWS magazine. She and husband Don led Good News' General Conference ministry from 1980 through 1992. She was a gifted writer, speaker, and leader, and helped bring the Marriage Enrichment program to the United Methodist Church. Virginia died at Lake Junaluska in January of 2004.

Dr. Edmund W. Robb, Jr. was another Life-time Honorary Board Member of Good News and a former chairman of our board. Ed was one of the great United Methodist leaders of the last 50 years. He helped launch A Foundation for Theological Education, the Institute on Religion and Democracy, and served as an approved United Methodist evangelist for more than 35 years. In 2000, Good News established the *Edmund W. Robb, Jr. United Methodist Renewal Award*, and presented it initially to Ed in recognition of his significant contribution on behalf of renewal within the United Methodist Church. Ed died in December of 2004.

Dr. William H. Hinson served for 18 years as pastor of First United Methodist Church in Houston, Texas. By any measure, Bill was one of the outstanding pastors in America—of any communion. Under his ministry at First United Methodist Church, Houston, the congregation received almost 8,500 members. Bill was a friend of and voice for the poor. He was also one of the most gifted communicators of the Gospel in our generation. He was a courageous leader in United Methodist renewal efforts and was chairman of the board of the Confessing Movement within the United Methodist Church when he died in December of 2004.

Mrs. Diane L. Knippers served on the staff of the Institute on Religion and Democracy for 23 years, the last twelve years as president. Diane was one of the most highly-respected leaders among all of those involved in mainline renewal and was considered a theological and intellectual heavyweight by those on both sides the theological aisle. *Time* magazine included Diane in its list of the 25 most-influential evangelicals in America—a list that included such well-known leaders as Billy and Franklin Graham, James Dobson, and Chuck Colson. She died in April of 2005.

The Rev. Robert D. Snyder served for more than fifty years as a pastor and evangelical leader in the East Ohio Conference and in 1969 was one of the founders of the East Ohio Evangelical Fellowship in that conference. He remained actively involved as a leader in that fellowship for many years, even after retiring as a pastor. Bob was a friend, mentor, and source of encouragement to hundreds of pastors and laity in the East Ohio Conference. Three times he chaired a national Good News Convocation and was a Lifetime Honorary Member of the Good News board. He was also a recipient of the *Edmund W. Robb, Jr. United Methodist Renewal Award*. Bob was another who was respected by those on both sides of the theological aisle. I often referred to Bob affectionately, but also with some seriousness, as "the Bishop of East Ohio." Bob died in August of 2005.

And last, Dr. David A. Seamands was a friend of all the renewal ministries in the United Methodist Church. David served as a United Methodist missionary, pastor, author, counselor, and seminary professor. He was a leader in the Evangelical Missions Council, which became an official part of Good News' ministry for eight years. He was one of the best, most thoughtful preachers in United Methodism. David was elected five times (1980-1996) as a delegate to General Conference. Several times he chaired strategic Minority Reports that became Majority Reports, which were then approved by delegates. The author of numerous books, David's *Healing for Damaged Emotions* alone sold more than a million copies. He, like several already mentioned, was a recipient of the *Edmund W. Robb, Jr. United Methodist Renewal Award*. David died in July of 2006.

These brothers and sisters in the ministry of renewal helped "Guard the good deposit" and their influence lives on. They were courageous and willing to stand boldly for the truth and to challenge error when necessary. The admonition that we are "surrounded by such a great cloud of witnesses" is more real to me than ever these days. And in occasional quiet moments, I think I could hear these friends saying to those of us who continue in the struggle, "Let us not become weary in doing good, for at the proper time we will reap a harvest if we do not give up" (Galatians 6:9). Thanks be to God for these friends—faithful servants and leaders in the renewal of the church.

James V. Heidinger II
Nicholasville, Kentucky
January 7, 2007

Part 1
DOCTRINE, DISSENT, AND DEFINITION

ONE

John Stott on evangelicalism and mainline renewal

An evangelical, says Stott, is an ordinary Christian who stands "in the mainstream of historic, orthodox, biblical Christianity."

David Brooks, *New York Times* columnist, wrote a few years ago that if evangelicals were to choose a pope, they would likely select Anglican pastor/theologian, John Stott. He may be right.

Stott, now 85, was interviewed in the October issue of *Christianity Today*, the publication's splendid 50th Anniversary issue. Stott has been a pivotal figure in evangelical renewal in the United Kingdom.

As pastor of All Soul's Church in London, Stott has made his mark on the evangelical world by his many books, commentaries, and sermons. He chaired committees that drafted the Lausanne Covenant in 1974 and the Manila Manifesto in 1989, two defining statements for evangelicals. He's been a long-time friend of Billy Graham.

For more than 35 years, Stott has devoted three months each year to travel the globe, ministering, and learning about churches in the two-thirds world.

He has timely words for us about evangelicalism, preaching, missions, and holiness for all who are concerned about renewal in the mainline.

What is evangelicalism? An evangelical, says Stott, is an ordinary Christian who stands "in the mainstream of historic, orthodox, biblical Christianity." This means, he adds, that "we can recite the Apostles Creed and the Nicene Creed without crossing our fingers." He is referring to British and American pastors who cross their fingers while saying the creeds, believing them irrelevant, suitable only for the dust bins of history.

Stott adds that "what God has *said* in Christ and in the biblical witness to Christ, and what God has *done* in and through Christ, are both...once and for all. There is a finality about God's *word* in Christ, and...about God's *work* in Christ. To imagine that we could add a word to his word, or add a work to his work, is extremely derogatory to the unique glory of our Lord Jesus Christ." He says simply, "Canonicity is apostolicity."

Stott was ordained 61 years ago. Back then, evangelicals in the Church of England "were a despised and rejected minority. The bishops lost no opportunity to ridicule us," he noted. While often frustrated and at variance with their church, both Stott and long-time colleague, J. I. Packer, resisted the urge to leave. They have been articulate, prolific witnesses, with the result that perhaps a fourth of the Church of England is now evangelical.

What about missions? Stott affirms short-term mission teams and believes they are, on the whole, "a good thing." He then adds, "But...this is only a very limited experience of cross-cultural mission." Speaking from years of travel, he cautions, "If God calls you to be a cross-cultural missionary, it will take you ten years to learn the language and to learn the culture in such a way that you are accepted more or less as a national."

This is timely. Recently, our church's mission board reported a dozen or so US-2 missionaries being commissioned and sent—for a two year stint, most all, I believe, to serve in the U.S. But I was saddened to hear about a long-term, career United Methodist missionary couple, with years of effective service overseas, whose contract was not renewed by the missions board. What used to be a robust, full-time overseas missions force of 1,500 continues to dwindle and is last reported at 247—and many of that number are not presently on the field. (By comparison, the Mission Society in Norcross, Georgia, has almost 200 missionaries overseas.)

What about preaching? Stott readily confesses, "I'm an impenitent believer in the importance of preaching." Of course, that's biblical preaching. He believes that churches live, grow, and flourish by the Word of God. (United Methodists, take note!) I was reminded of this when a friend told of his visit recently to hear the Rev. Adam Hamilton at the Church of the Resurrection (UMC) in Kansas City—where more than 8,000 worship each Sunday. Adam's sermon, he said, was 35 minutes long and sometimes is 45 minutes long. And he's always scriptural. But many United Methodists today report that their pastor preaches just seven or eight minutes—barely a sermonette. And be sure of this: sermonettes will make us Christianettes. Pastors must learn to *expound* the Word of God, not dissect, denigrate, and deny it. (Frankly, I'm weary of hearing about pastors who criticize, correct, and update the Apostle Paul.)

Stott holds these convictions: God wants his church to grow; it grows by the Word of God; and the Word of God comes to the people of God mainly, though not exclusively, through preaching.

What about holiness? Stott says he sees an absence of the quest for scriptural holiness among evangelicals today. He admits the term sometimes sounds sanctimonious. But he reminds us, "The holiness of the New Testament is Christlikeness." He longs for evangelicals "to grow in Christlikeness such as is described in Galatians 5:22-23."

What a timely word for us United Methodists. Wesley believed holiness or Christian perfection was the grand *depositum* God gave to the Methodists. Where this was not preached, he said, "believers grow dead and cold."

My advice? Get Stott's books and read them. Then, read them again.

November/December 2006

TWO

Thinking about our working theology

We have heard repeatedly that the gospel is the "good news of God's unconditional love. Now let us go out and love one another in the same way." This admonition, however, can be cruel if we don't help folks come to grips with the human condition of sin that makes it impossible for us to just "go out and love one another."

Philip Turner, an Episcopalian, is the former Dean of the Berkeley Divinity School at Yale. He also served ten years as a missionary in Uganda and returned to do graduate work in Christian Ethics with Paul Ramsey at Princeton University.

Writing in an issue of *First Things* ("An Unworkable Theology," June/July 2005), Turner noted the difference in the Episcopal Church's theological articles, liturgies, and confessional statements compared to what he called his church's "working theology." To find the working theology, he says, one must review the resolutions passed at official gatherings and listen to what clergy say Sunday by Sunday from the pulpit.

His piece haunted me. As he describes the "working theology" of many Episcopalians, he sounded like he was writing about us United Methodists, too. Look at what he says about his experience.

Upon completion of his graduate work, Turner taught at the Episcopal Theological Seminary of the Southwest. He writes of his excitement as he listened to his first student sermon "only to be taken aback by its vacuity." The student asked the right question, "What is the Christian gospel?" But his answer throughout the sermon was simply "God is love. God loves us. We, therefore, ought to love one another."

Stunned by the shallowness, Turner writes "I waited in vain for some word about the saving power of Christ's cross or the declaration of God's victory in Christ's resurrection. I waited in vain for a promise of the Holy Spirit. I waited in vain also for an admonition to wait patiently and faithfully for the Lord's return. I waited in vain for a call to repentance and amendment of life in accord with the pattern of Christ's life."

The rich content of preaching he had heard for a decade in Anglican pulpits in Uganda was simply not there. Nor was this an isolated incident. Over the years, he added, "I have heard the same sermon preached from pulpit after pulpit by experienced priests."

Unfortunately, so have many United Methodists. We have heard repeatedly that the gospel is the "good news of God's unconditional love. Now let us go out and love one another in the same way." This admonition, however, can be cruel if we don't help folks come to grips with the human condition of sin that makes it impossible for us to just "go out and love one another."

The working theology of the Episcopal Church, writes Turner, begins with the claim that "God is love, pure and simple. Thus, one is to see in Christ's death no judgment upon the human condition. Rather, one is to see an affirmation of creation and the persons we are. The life and death of Jesus reveal the fact that God accepts and affirms us." This sounds plausible at first, but it is classic half-truth. Indeed, God loves us while we are yet sinners, but he calls us to repentance, new life, and holy living.

From a simplistic understanding of God, we move to a further conclusion, Turner says about the Episcopalians "working theology." "God wants us to love one another, and such love requires of us both acceptance and affirmation of the other.... Accepting love requires a form of justice that is inclusive of all people, particularly those who in some way have been marginalized by oppressive social practice. The mission of the Church is, therefore, to see that those who have been rejected are included—for justice as inclusion defines public policy." The result of all this, Turner claims, is "a practical equivalence between the gospel of the Kingdom of God and a particular form of social justice." For many in the Episcopal Church he says, the gospel has been equated with the social justice concept of "radical inclusion."

So, what we are seeing today in the Episcopal Church (and the other mainline denominations as well, he adds) is not simply an ethical divide about the "rightness or wrongness of homosexuality and same-sex marriage. It's a theological chasm—one that separates those who hold a theology of divine *acceptance* from those who hold a theology of divine *redemption*" (emphasis his). This new theology of "divine acceptance" no longer needs terms such as faith, justification, repentance, and holiness of life. These terms "belong to an antique vocabulary that must be outgrown or reinterpreted," he says.

This leaves only one kind of witness, writes Turner—the inclusion of the previously excluded. God has already included everybody, and now we ought to do the same. The new message, then, amounts to "inclusion *without qualification*" (emphasis his).

This "working theology" of many contemporary Episcopalians (and many liberal Protestants as well, he suggests) is far from the basic content of "Nicene Christianity." In fact, he concludes, "It is a theology which most Anglicans in the rest of the world no longer recognize as Christian."

July/August 2005

THREE

The cure for what ails us

The biblical scholars involved in the oft-cited "Jesus Seminar" are theologians whose presuppositions are that Jesus was something other than what the gospel accounts present him to be. That's where they begin.

The ministry of Good News was launched 38 years ago. From the very beginning, our concerns have always been theological. Whether the focus was on curriculum, confirmation materials, or "theological pluralism," we have attempted to encourage our church to rediscover its Wesleyan doctrinal heritage—what Wesley called Scriptural Christianity.

While pastoring in East Ohio years ago, I remember conference meetings in which we discussed vigorously our United Methodist membership loss and the need for greater evangelistic outreach. As various programs and strategies were considered as hopeful remedies, I wondered if new and better signs, more contemporary music, friendlier greeters, and better public relations, etc. really would cure what ailed us. Instead, I feared that perhaps we had simply failed to communicate effectively the authentic message of the gospel.

Many years ago, former Candler School of Theology Prof. John Lawson wrote, "The evangelical renewal of the church cannot arise apart from a renewal of her historic and scriptural evangelical theology" (*An Evangelical Faith for Today*, Abingdon). He was right.

In 1999, a group of respected evangelicals including Timothy George, Maxie Dunnam, Thomas Oden, and J. I. Packer released "The Gospel of Jesus Christ: An Evangelical Celebration" in *Christianity Today*. It was an attempt to say "This is what the good news really is!" David Neff, executive editor of *Christianity Today*, writing for the drafting committee, noted the infinite capacity of human beings for "getting things wrong," even the substance of the gospel. He added that as evangelicals interact with the historic churches, we realize that "the biblical understanding of the good news is, first, *the most important thing that we can offer friends in these churches* and, second, *the only thing in which we can find true unity*" (emphasis mine).

Refreshingly, it declared: "This Gospel is the only Gospel; there is no other; and to change its substance is to pervert and indeed destroy it." In a series of affirmations and denials, the document stated, "We affirm that the bodily resurrection of Christ from the dead is essential to the biblical gospel (1 Corinthians 15:14). We deny the validity of any so-called gospel that denies the historical reality of the bodily resurrection of Christ." No waffling or ambiguity there.

In one of the chapters of *Ancient & Postmodern Christianity*, a book of essays in honor of Thomas C. Oden, Lutheran theologian Carl E. Braaten grapples with the critical theological disputes of the twentieth century. Let me highlight three of those conflicts.

First, Braaten presents the quest for the "historical Jesus." The thrust of this movement was to go behind the gospels to get at Jesus as he really was. The result was a picture of Jesus as simply a heroic personality "at odds with the way the Evangelists portrayed Jesus as the Christ." The outcome was a "so-called historical Jesus" fashioned to suit modern sensibilities, and not the real living Jesus Christ of apostolic preaching.

Braaten believes we are currently "witnessing a revival of the quest of the historical Jesus. The result is virtually the same. The historical Jesus in the works of the current crop of questers is totally void of gospel significance, whether it be that of [Robert] Funk, [John Dominc] Crossan, [Marcus] Borg or [John Shelby] Spong."

The problem here is one of presuppositions, says Braaten. "If we presuppose that Jesus is someone else than his best friends and followers said he was, we will discover a Jesus we have never known—a complete stranger to the gospel." And we will end up answering Jesus' question, "And who do you say that I am?" in whatever way we may choose.

Braaten declares: "The real Jesus is the core of the gospel. He is the ground and content of faith, who can be truly known only by the testimony of the Holy Spirit. The real Jesus of history is the risen Christ; we cannot have one without the other. They belong indivisibly and inseparably together, as the creed of Chalcedon has taught us to say."

The biblical scholars involved in the oft-cited "Jesus Seminar" are theologians whose *presuppositions* are that Jesus was something *other than* what the gospel accounts present him to be. That's where they begin.

Second, Braaten presents Rudolf Bultmann and the hermeneutical question. One cannot overstate the impact of this German theologian on American Protestant theology in the last century. In a Good News dialogue with curriculum personnel in Nashville years ago, a denominational leader leaned back with arms folded and affirmed to the group, "Now, we all know that everyone today affirms the Bultmannian view of Scripture." Of course, not everyone did, but it reflects how popular Bultmann was for several generations of clergy.

Bultmann tried to build a bridge from the first century *preaching* to twentieth century *experience*. He was trying to make the ancient faith appear acceptable to modern and scientific people. To do this, Bultmann "laid all the stress on the existential (personal faith experience) meaning of the gospel rather than get bogged down in the debatable facts of history." Bultmann would say, "An historical fact which involves a resurrection from the dead is utterly inconceivable." In Bultmann's understanding, historical facts and existential meaning simply are oil and water—they do not mix.

The problem, says Braaten, is that "without the narrative history of Jesus, there would be no gospel in the Gospels. There must be a fundamental continuity between the Christ of faith in whom we believe and the historical Jesus." I vividly recall a conversation with a college classmate years ago who, after attending a liberal seminary, told me that it would not disturb his faith if the bones of Jesus were one day found in the Holy Land. What was important, he insisted, was "resurrection faith," not an empty tomb.

Third, Braaten mentions Wolfhart Pannenberg and reclaiming the historical resurrection. Pannenberg had a major impact on Thomas C. Oden, helping him in his reversal from being a Bultmannian to affirming the historicity of the resurrection. The first lecture Pannenberg delivered when he came to America was titled "Did Jesus Really Rise from the Dead?" His answer was yes, to the surprise of many. After all, Bultmann had declared, "The resurrection itself is not an event of past history." But Pannenberg had the courage to call the bluff of these theologians. He insisted that the truth of the gospel rested on two conditions: "that it really happened to Jesus and that it means what the first witnesses said it meant." An Easter "*experience*" means nothing without the Easter "*event*"—the resurrection of Jesus.

Revisiting these conflicts, says Braaten, should remind us "to keep the gospel at the flaming center of all our thinking and writing...lest the gospel be controlled by alien ideologies, some isms out there that keep our theological legs moving on the treadmill of the latest trends." He added that we also "should reverse the trend in theological education that has turned the pyramid of profound learning on its head, giving greater time and attention to what is recent and novel at the expense of what is ancient and classical."

Our task, he says in conclusion, is "to teach the basics all over again, and help every new generation to learn them by heart and love them with a passion." Might it be that United Methodism will begin "to teach the basics all over again?" It would surely be the cure for what ails us.

May/June 2005

FOUR

Tom Oden's remarkable journey

In his own words, Oden admits, "I left seminary
having learned to treat Scripture selectively...
I adapted the Bible to my ideology—an ideology
of social and political change largely shaped by
soft Marxist premises about history and a
romanticized vision of the emerging power
and virtue of the underclass."

While preparing my remarks to present the Fifth Annual Edmund W. Robb, Jr. Award to Dr. Tom Oden, I read again the account of Tom's theological "reversal" found in his book, *The Rebirth of Orthodoxy*. It should be required reading for all United Methodist seminarians.

Oden, who retired last year from 33 years of teaching at Drew University School of Theology, was a consistent Bultmannian until about 1966. That is, he believed the resurrection occurred in the memory of the disciples, but not in history.

In his own words, Oden admits "I left seminary having learned to treat Scripture selectively...I adapted the Bible to my ideology—an ideology of social and political change largely shaped by soft Marxist premises about history and a romanticized vision of the emerging power and virtue of the underclass."

Tom refers to himself as having been a "movement" theologian in his early years. He had made his bed with such trendy movements as United World Federalists promoting world government, liberalized abortion, the demythologizing movement (about which he did his PhD dissertation), Transactional Analysis, parapsychology, biorhythm charts, tarot cards, and the list goes on.

About this obsession, Oden says, "The shocker is not merely that

I rode so many bandwagons, but that I thought I was doing Christian teaching a marvelous favor by it and at times considered this accommodation the very substance of the Christian teaching office."

Two persons had a major impact on Oden. In 1966, he spent time with Wolfhart Pannenburg, and in 1973, he met Will Herberg, his Jewish mentor and elder colleague at Drew. It was Herberg who said bluntly to Oden, "Tom, you have not yet met the great minds of your own tradition. Just as I, after my Communist days, found it decisive to read the Talmud and the Midrashim carefully to discover who I was as a Jew, you will have to sit at the feet of the ancient Christian writers to discover who you are as a possible person of faith. Without solid textual grounding, you will become lost in supposed relevance." Until you begin to do this, Herberg added pointedly, "you are not a theologian except in name, even if remunerated as one."

About those pointed words, Oden says, "I was stunned. He had nailed me."

Until then, Oden had not dreamed he would ever one day grant to Scripture its own distinctive premises—that is, divine sovereignty, revelation, incarnation, resurrection, and final judgment. "I had been taught that these premises were precisely what had to be transcended, reworded, circumvented, and danced around in order to communicate with the modern mind."

Many of us have heard these very sentiments a thousand times.

Oden's radical theological conversion actually took place incrementally, in quiet reading as he immersed himself in classic orthodox writings, plus long conversations with his students. "Once blown by every wind of doctrine and preoccupied with therapeutic fads amid the spirit of hypertoleration, I came to grasp the consensual reasoning that occurs so effortlessly within classic Christianity."

What was it that changed the course of Oden's life? In his words, "A simple reversal that hung on a single pivot: attentiveness to the text of Scripture, especially as viewed by its early consensual interpreters" (emphasis mine). As an aside of personal confession, Oden writes, "I am recognizing a fair amount of self-delusion and demonic deception in ideologies that once appeared to me seductive."

In a powerful comparison of "then and now," Oden writes, "Then I distrusted even the faint smell of orthodoxy. I was in love with heresy—the wilder, the more seductive. Now I have come to trust the very consensus I once dismissed and distrusted. I now relish studying the diverse rainbow of orthodox voices from varied cultures spanning all continents over two thousand years."

Out of the dregs of his obsessive faddism came his growing distaste for novelty, heresy, pretense, and messianic idealism. Oden is now totally committed to "unoriginality." And he means it. "That is not a joke but a solemn pledge. I am trying to curb any pretense at 'improving' upon the apostles and fathers."

Some of Oden's old friends still wonder why he changed his mind. Tom replies kindly, "I suspect that they will never get it. The irony is that I changed only by moving closer to that which is unchanging."

Oden's remarkable journey reminds us that the church's greatest challenge may not come from those outside who oppose and ridicule the gospel, but from those within who would change it.

March/April 2005

FIVE

Doctrine and the people called Methodists

The move away from doctrine during this period also provided natural cover for pastors who were being trained in the emerging liberal theology. Many could surrender the supernatural elements of apostolic faith — the virgin birth, the deity and miracles of Jesus, and his bodily resurrection — and continue on in ministry without ever having to talk much about those things. Social ministry was in, theological definition was out.

Debate has been renewed in recent months about the role of doctrine for United Methodists. What is the place, for example, of orthodox Christian doctrine in our church? For years we have heard that we are not a creedal church; that Methodists have been more interested in "faith working through love;" that Methodists have always been more experiential than doctrinal; that doctrine should not be the basis for juridical action or for coercion.

There is truth in some of this, no doubt. In 1952, the bishops of the Methodist Church said in addressing that year's General Conference that "Our theology has never been a closely organized doctrinal system. We have never insisted on uniformity of thought or statement." However, the bishops went on to say in that address, "There are great Christian doctrines which we most surely hold and firmly believe." Commenting on this address, Bishop Nolan B. Harmon said, "Methodists have always heatedly rejected the idea that Methodism is simply a 'movement' with no formal doctrine" (*Understanding the United Methodist Church*, Abingdon, 1974).

A brief history of the non-creedal claims

The oral tradition claiming Methodism to be a non-creedal church has a history that reaches back at least to the early 1900s, the time of the fundamentalist/modernist controversy. Methodism, at that time, had just experienced the unpleasant controversy about its holiness message. General Conference took action in 1894 to bring holiness evangelists under the church's strict control. Many left Methodism to form no less than ten different holiness groups. They believed the Methodist Church was not being faithful to Wesley's understanding of sanctification and perfect love.

In the face of the bitter controversy beginning to brew over the fundamentalist/modernist debate, Methodism was determined to avoid more division. The result was that Methodism moved even further away from careful creedal and doctrinal formulation to a mood of greater openness, tolerance, and emphasis on Christian love in action. There was also the feeling that with so many urgent social ills in America's growing cities, theological debate might prevent the church from meeting human needs.

This led to a growing antipathy toward creeds, a pattern that can be seen in the periodical literature of 1910-1920. The trend clearly was to shift focus from creeds to human needs. A. H. Goodenough wrote in the *Methodist Review* in November, 1910: "Creeds have had their day. They are no longer effective. Without doubt, they were well intended. Possibly they have done some good—they certainly have done much harm. The church has been loyal to her creeds, and has spent much good blood and splendid brains in the defense of them. All this was considered the very essence of Christianity. It was child's play, as we now see it, and in some instances paganism.... The creeds are retired to the museums and labeled 'Obsolete.'"

Seeing division and strife around them from the fundamentalist/modernist controversy, Methodists were more than ready to relax their attention on creedal and doctrinal formulation. One New York pastor, Philip Frick, wrote with near exhilaration an article entitled, "Why the Methodist Church Is So Little Disturbed by the Fundamentalist Controversy," (*Methodist Review*, 1924), in which he gives the reason as being Methodism's lack of dogmatic creedal assertion.

Further evidence of the growing antipathy to creedal formulation at this time can be seen in the change in requirements for membership.

In 1864, the Methodist Episcopal Church required members to subscribe to the Articles of Religion. This requirement was removed in 1916. Belief in the Apostles' Creed continued to be required after 1924 as it was included in the baptismal ritual, but it, too, was dropped in 1932.

It may well have been in response to General Conference's dropping of the Apostles' Creed in 1932, as well as the popular preference for using the new Social Creed rather than theological creeds, that led to Edwin Lewis' article of alarm over "The Fatal Apostasy of the Modern Church." Lewis, a professor of systematic theology at Drew Theological Seminary, wrote stinging words in response to these changes: "But what does the modern church believe? The church is becoming creedless as rapidly as the innovators can have their way. The 'Confession of Faith'—what is happening to it? Or what about the 'new' confessions that one sees and hears—suitable enough, one imagines, for, say, a fraternal order. And as for the Apostles' Creed—'our people will not say it any more': which means, apparently, that 'our people, having some difficulties over the virgin birth and the resurrection of the body, have elected the easy way of believing in nothing at all—certainly not in "the Holy Catholic Church"'" (*Religion in Life*, Autumn, 1933).

So this era saw a transition from doctrinal and theological concerns to a growing new interest in, if not preoccupation with, social ministry. The church focused not on the content of belief, for that could be divisive, but rather upon Christian love in action through social ministry. This inattention to theology may have been partially responsible for Methodism's tragic susceptibility to the influence of liberal theology and German philosophy that were rapidly finding a home in our Methodist seminaries.

The move away from doctrine during this period also provided natural cover for pastors who were being trained in the emerging liberal theology. Many could surrender the supernatural elements of apostolic faith—the virgin birth, the deity and miracles of Jesus, and his bodily resurrection—and continue on in ministry without ever having to talk much about those things. Social ministry was in, theological definition was out.

This helps us understand the oral tradition that has come down to us today. It is this: United Methodism is not a creedal church, we live in a changing world, and doctrines we used to teach may not be relevant today. And most recently, folks in one of our annual conferences were warned by letter of a "movement away from an evolving and ever-changing understanding of God guided by the Holy Spirit." Of course, "an evolving and ever-changing understanding of God" could never be expressed in a creed or traditional formulation, for it would be forever changing. The best folks might get would be a list of "Affirmations of the month," but not "the faith once for all delivered to the saints" (Jude 3).

Looking again at our Wesleyan tradition

But is the oral tradition really our Wesleyan theological tradition? One senses we have done violence to both Wesley and American Methodism with such sloppiness and ambiguity.

Charles Yrigoyen, Jr., in his helpful book *Belief Matters*, reminds us that the church's doctrine helps us understand the biblical message in a "clearer, holistic, more organized way," and thus we can communicate it more effectively. Unfortunately, many United Methodists today don't really understand that message. He also reminds us that the official doctrine of the church "protects us from false and subversive teachings." Pastors have the responsibility to feed their flocks and make sure they are not grazing in toxic pastures.

Belief certainly mattered to John Wesley, despite the claims of his revisionists. Wesley insisted on doctrinal faithfulness. In 1763 Wesley drafted a Model Deed which stipulated that the pulpits of the Methodist chapels were to be used by those persons who preached only those doctrines contained in Wesley's New Testament notes and his four volumes of sermons. If a preacher didn't conform, he was replaced within three months. Wesley would never have shrugged off reports of an errant preacher by saying, as do many today, "Well, we Methodists think and let think." (He did say that, of course, in "The Character of a Methodist," but let's quote his entire sentence: "But as to all opinions which do not strike at the root of Christianity, we think and let think.")

While Wesley had a refreshing breadth of spirit about him, there were doctrines he viewed as essential to the faith. Robert Chiles, concurring with Methodist theologian Colin Williams, lists the doctrines that Wesley insisted on at various times in his ministry as "original sin, the deity of Christ, the atonement, justification by faith alone, the work of the Holy Spirit (including new birth and holiness), and the Trinity" (Chiles citing Colin Williams, *John Wesley's Theology Today*). This is simply apostolic Christianity.

Yes, we United Methodists take doctrine very seriously. Each person seeking to become a clergy member within our denomination is asked, "(8) Have you studied the doctrines of the United Methodist Church? (9) After full examination, do you believe that our doctrines are in harmony with the Holy Scriptures? (10) Will you preach and maintain them?" (*Book of Discipline*, Par. 327). Candidates are expected to answer in the affirmative.

The church, in fact, takes doctrine seriously enough that a bishop, clergy member, local pastor, or diaconal minister may be charged formally with "dissemination of doctrines contrary to the established standards of doctrine of the United Methodist Church" (*Discipline*, Par. 2624.1f), which can lead to a trial. Doctrine is not tangential to the people called Methodists.

Alister McGrath, professor at Oxford, has warned that "Inattention to doctrine robs a church of her reason for existence, and opens the way to enslavement and oppression by the world." Certainly, attention to doctrine will help United Methodists understand that our doctrinal standards are not, have never been, and must never be, "evolving and ever-changing." That would be a guarantor of continued confusion and further decline.

September/October 2003

SIX

Are there any theological boundaries?

Rhett Jackson said, "we do not believe in the virgin birth, physical resurrection, ancient creeds or any of the other magic revealed in much of our liturgy and literature." He admits reading John A.T. Robinson's Honest to God *decades ago, which changed him dramatically.*

When I entered the ministry in 1967, I remember being struck by how reluctant pastors were to talk theology. Thirty-five years later, I think I understand the reluctance. More United Methodists than we might imagine no longer affirm the substance of classic Christian doctrine. Today, more folks are willing to admit it openly. Consider two recent situations:

Example One. Rhett Jackson, a layman from South Carolina, lamented in a commentary in the *United Methodist Reporter* that he was a part of a group in his church seeking a "religion of reason." Their problem, said Jackson, a delegate to 42 Annual Conferences and eight General Conferences, is that "we do not believe in the virgin birth, physical resurrection, ancient creeds, or any of the other magic revealed in much of our liturgy and literature." He admits reading John A. T. Robinson's *Honest to God* decades ago, which changed him dramatically.

In the conclusion of this tragic article, he says, "I have always admired our broad theological umbrella, but if the Confession [Confessing] Movement and Good News folks own 60 percent of this umbrella, I will have to walk away." (Note, by the way, that his "broad theological umbrella" is not compatible with a strong evangelical presence.)

Example Two. In a speech January 28, 2002 at Iliff School of Theology in Denver, Bishop Joe Sprague (Northern Illinois) shared with students there "candidly and vulnerably" about just who "Jesus the risen Christ is for me." In his message, Sprague denied the classic understandings of Jesus' full and unique deity, virgin birth, blood atonement, and physical [bodily] resurrection. To believe these, he cautions, is "idolatry."

Sprague warned the students against a "christocentric exclusivism" which believes that Jesus is the only way to God's "gift of salvation." Such a view, he says, is "arrogant," and we assume then, unchristian. Sprague also denied the traditional Christian understanding that Christ died on the cross for the sins of all humanity. When asked about the uniqueness of Jesus, Sprague responded, "Is it possible for another? I would have to leave that possibility open." Sprague seems to have no orthodox arrows left in his theological quiver. Not only does he abandon two millenia of historic Christian doctrine, he charges those of us who are orthodox and evangelical as being idolaters.

These examples remind us we have critical differences in the United Methodist Church about the substance of our faith. This debate is not new. In the early 1900s, America's mainline churches began surrendering their supernatural substance in order to accommodate the new intellectual currents of the day. Harold Paul Sloan, a pastor from New Jersey, organized a resistance effort against this trend called The Methodist League for Faith and Life. In the late 1920s, he wrote to Bishop Raymond Wade with deep concern about Methodism's doctrinal defection: "I am profoundly convinced that the Methodist Church is waiting for the leadership of the Board of Bishops....We can have no revival unless the Bishops aggressively proclaim their undeviating confidence in the deity, virgin birth, and bodily resurrection of Jesus Christ." This is a relevant plea for today.

In the early 1930s, Edwin Lewis, professor at the Theology School at Drew University, protested Methodism's doctrinal trend, charging that the church "is becoming creedless." Citing the Apostles' Creed, Lewis wrote of pastors complaining that "our people will not say it any more," having difficulties over the virgin birth and the resurrection of the body. Similar denials of core doctrine are found in later theologians such as Rudolph Bultmann, John A. T. Robinson, John Hick, and more recently Episcopal Bishop John Spong and Prof. Marcus Borg, two theologians whom Bishop Sprague says he admires.

We are left, then, with serious questions. How far astray can an active UM bishop go, theologically, before that bishop's teaching becomes unacceptable for our United Methodist Council of Bishops, the body charged with defending, teaching, and proclaiming the church's evangelical faith? Are there any limits? Would *any* errant teaching *ever* merit a rebuke or even a heresy trial? Also, what can we do about our seminaries, some of which may still be teaching a deconstructionist, "Jesus Seminar" theology that sounds Christian but has little, if any, Christian substance? This neutered gospel about a domesticated deity was clearly not the faith of the apostles and martyrs.

The issue is not whether Bishop Sprague and others are nice persons or sincere. Obviously, they are. The issue is one of boundaries, accountability, and faithfulness. John R. W. Stott said it well: "We live in the twentieth century, but we are tethered to the first. What Jesus Christ said and did was unique and final. So is the interpretative teaching of the apostles, His chosen eyewitnesses and ambassadors."

When we move away from apostolic teaching, we have a new religion—it is no longer classic Christianity. And that makes it a very serious matter.

September/October 2002

SEVEN

Bishop Spong and the deconstruction of Christianity

The late Canon Michael Green asked an important question in The Truth of God Incarnate *published years ago: "How much can you remove from a car, and still possess what is properly called a car?" He says lights may be a luxury and brakes may be dispensed with, but if you remove the engine or chassis, are you still talking about a car at all?*

"The Christian church doesn't really believe what it claims to believe," said the smiling Muslim evangelist to a bewildered Nigerian Christian. "One of their bishops even admits so! Here's a book that proves it. It's called *The Resurrection: Myth or Reality?* by someone named Spong. He's a Christian bishop."

Thus begins the book *Can A Bishop Be Wrong?*, a volume in which ten Episcopalian theologians (including two bishops) unite to say they believe Episcopal Bishop John Shelby Spong "has essentially placed himself outside the Christian tradition and is using his privileged position as a bishop to attack it."

Why is this important for us United Methodists? Because John Spong has been traveling the United Methodist circuit recently speaking and being applauded as something of a celebrity.

During Palm Sunday weekend (2002), Spong gave four addresses at the Dilworth United Methodist Church in Charlotte, North Carolina. On Friday evening, some 500 persons paid $15 each to hear his revisionisms. At the conclusion, the winsome and articulate bishop received a standing ovation.

A month earlier, Spong was a featured speaker along with United Methodist Bishops Judy Craig (retired) and Sharon Zimmerman Rader

(Wisconsin Area), at the "Kairos CoMotion" Conference in Madison, Wisconsin. Several years ago, Spong gave five lectures to pastors at United Methodist-related McKendree College in southern Illinois on the theme of the "Resurrection," in which he does not believe.

Now, I can hear some of you saying, "Wait a moment. We live in a multicultural, diverse world. Let's cut the bishop some slack here!"

But the late Canon Michael Green asked an important question in *The Truth of God Incarnate*, published years ago: "How much can you remove from a car, and still possess what is properly called a car?" He says lights may be a luxury and brakes may be dispensed with, but if you remove the engine or chassis, are you still talking about a car at all?

It seems that John Spong has completely dismantled the Christian car, doctrinally. Read just a few of his 12 Theses, which he posted on his Diocese of Newark website:

• Theism, as a way of defining God, is dead. So most theological God-talk is today meaningless. A new way to speak of God must be found.

• Since God can no longer be conceived in theistic terms, it becomes nonsensical to seek to understand Jesus as the incarnation of the theistic deity. So the Christology of the ages is bankrupt.

• The virgin birth, understood as literal biology, makes Christ's divinity, as traditionally understood, impossible.

• The miracle stories of the New Testament can no longer be interpreted...as supernatural events performed by an incarnate deity.

• The view of the cross as the sacrifice for the sins of the world is a barbarian idea based on primitive concepts of God and must be dismissed. [So much for glorying in the Cross of Christ.]

There are more, but you get the drift. Spong told the "Kairos CoMotion" crowd of 300 that Jesus couldn't have ascended, he would have gone into orbit. His beliefs have become so heretical that no less than 50 Bishops of the Episcopal Church USA disassociated themselves from Spong in a public declaration in 1998. They charged, "In no way do [Spong's theses] represent the doctrine, discipline, or worship of the Episcopal Church—or any other branch of orthodox Christianity."

Several things are disturbing about all this. First, that John Spong is getting such easy entree to United Methodist audiences, even though he has jettisoned the entire substance of classic Christian doctrine.

Second, it should be troubling that United Methodist Bishops Craig and Rader joined so freely in the de-constructionist fun in Madison.

Downplaying the "ancient creeds," Bishop Craig said, "We are saying of the tradition and orthodoxy that it is the heresy." She added that she preferred to live in "a tradition that is new every day." (That phrase, by the way, seems contradictory.) Bishop Rader said, "We've been warned not to talk openly about sexuality. We've been warned not to say that the *Book of Discipline* is sometimes incompatible with Christian teaching. We've been warned not to tell that we are gay or lesbian."

These views which denigrate the Christian tradition and our *Book of Discipline* are disturbing to hear from two of our United Methodist bishops. It's troubling because our bishops are charged specifically "To guard, transmit, teach, and proclaim, corporately and individually, the apostolic faith as it is expressed in Scripture and tradition...." (Par. 414.3, *Discipline*). Quite simply, bishops are to guard and teach the church's "tradition," not define it as "the heresy."

This brings us United Methodists back to the charge made by the Muslim evangelist. Does the United Methodist Church really believe what it claims to believe?

May/June 2002

EIGHT

Some unfinished business

The view of an expanded or open revelation is found in the writings of some radical feminists. Rosemary Radford Ruether, for instance, holds that feminist theology cannot be done from the existing base of the Christian Bible. "Feminist theology must create a new textual base, a new canon," she says.

In 1997, 22 persons shared in an extraordinary dialogue. Eleven liberals and eleven evangelicals (so described by the sponsoring Commission) met in theological dialogue. Conversations were cordial but brought little unity. However, all agreed with Bishop Judith Craig's observation that there were "two divergent world views," when thinking of revelation and humanity.

The first view is that the "Holy Spirit's activity is such that we continue to receive new revelation from God" (the view of many theological liberals) while the other view "believes the Holy Spirit is active in helping us comprehend what has already been revealed" (the view of most evangelicals).

This is a question of enormous importance to the church. As the document "In Search of Unity," which emerged from the dialogue, states: "Others believe themselves to be recipients of new and expanded revelation from God that is beyond the canon of Scripture." Unfortunately, subsequent dialogues have failed to address this highly questionable claim.

The view of an expanded or open revelation is found in the writings of some radical feminists. Rosemary Radford Ruether, for instance, holds that feminist theology cannot be done from the existing base of the Christian Bible. "Feminist theology must create a new textual base, a new canon," she says. And Elisabeth Schussler

Fiorenza contends that: "The locus or place of divine revelation and grace is...not the Bible or the tradition of a patriarchal church, but the *ekklesia* of women and the lives of women...." Clearly, the Bible is not the authority for faith and practice for either.

Marcus Borg speaking at Perkins School of Theology's Laity Week, was reported as saying, "The Bible is the Word of God. Jesus is the Word of God. A person can be the Word of God. A book can be the Word." We might assume that a poem, story, or kind deed could be the Word of God. But something is terribly inadequate about that. One must inevitably ask, "Who is the final arbiter of what is considered the Word of God?" We become the judges. And nothing is normative.

The question of revelation and authority, of course, is not new. Many theologians have addressed this issue and are worth hearing. Consider:

- Leon Morris, Principal of Ridley College, in Melbourne, Australia, who has written: "There is a core of revelation by which we must abide. If we forsake it what is left is not Christianity....The essential Christian message is the good news of what God has done in Christ. Once that action has been performed there is no adding to it. The Bible is the book that bears the definitive witness to what God has done. Once that witness has been borne there is no adding to it, or, for that matter, subtracting from it" (*I Believe in Revelation*). Don't fiddle with the canon, he says.

- Anglican James I. Packer, who claims the only way to avoid the skeptical outcome of contemporary theology "is to return to the historic Christian doctrine...that Scripture is in its nature revealed truth in writing and an authoritative norm for human thought about God" (*Revelation and the Bible*). Packer says God reveals himself in historical events no less than in other ways, but the meaning of that revelation is obscure apart from the divine disclosure of its cognitive significance—that is, apart from propositional revelation. Thus the understanding by most all evangelicals that the Bible is the Word of God written.

- H. D. McDonald, who has written, "Further, by calling revelation 'historical,' stress is laid on the actuality of the events recorded in Scripture. The events are not simply projections of the religious consciousness onto history. The testimony of the Christian Church is that God revealed himself in human history, and now, in Scripture—in the very words and propositions of Scripture—God reveals himself" (*The New International Dictionary of the Christian Church*). This idea of God making himself known in both redemptive acts and utterances is not so much a biblical idea, as it is *the* biblical idea, he says.

- Prof. Oscar Cullmann wrote, "The teaching-office of the Church did not abdicate in this final act of fixing the canon, but made its future activity dependent on a superior norm" (*The Early Church*). Any future teaching and activity by the Church has always been seen as to be done within the context of the established canon.

The Church has never permitted its pastors and teachers "to be recipients of new and expanded revelation from God that is beyond the canon of scripture." Any such view of an open canon, it seems clear, would guarantee confusion, wrong teaching, and a disregard for the Church's historic doctrine—come to think of it, the very thing we are now experiencing.

May/June 2001

NINE

Preaching and teaching the truth

There remains no common or universal reference point of truth which is used as a guide. You have your truth; I have mine. In fact, any universal claim to truth is often criticized today because it supposedly excludes other views and even does "violence" to persons by marginalizing their views.

At the 1996 North Central Jurisdictional Conference, I witnessed the impressive service of consecration of four new bishops. Amidst the beauty and pageantry, I remember the power of the consecration liturgy: "As servants of the whole Church, you are called to preach and teach the truth of the gospel to all God's people." It asked, "Will you guard the faith, order, liturgy, doctrine, and discipline of the Church against all that is contrary to God's Word?"

Guard the faith. Teach the truth of the Gospel. We hear little about this today. For some reason, the church has forgotten that Jesus said, "...and you shall know the truth, and the truth will make you free" (John 8:32, RSV). Paul urged Timothy, "Do your best to present yourself to God as one approved, a workman who has no need to be ashamed, rightly handling the word of truth" (2 Timothy 2:15, RSV). The message we are to "rightly handle," let's remember, is "the word of truth."

How do we explain, then, the "Faith and Reason" video series available through United Methodist Communications and Ecu-Film, which features speakers who question our Lord's claims to deity? Included in the 24-video series are such notable Jesus Seminar participants such as Marcus Borg, Dominic Crossan, and other scholars who are ever ready to disclaim the historicity of the biblical narratives.

The series also uncritically examines the beliefs of the late Rev. D. L. Dykes, a United Methodist pastor who declared about Jesus, "He did not see himself as the Son of God, he didn't see himself as anything special." Dykes is also quoted as saying "Jesus is not God," and the Holy Trinity just isn't "important."

The fact is, this kind of mishandling of "the word of truth" is not new. Episcopal Bishop John Shelby Spong wrote in 1982, "Can we with integrity continue to support and engage in a missionary enterprise designed to convert?...I will not make any further attempt to convert the Buddhist, the Jew, the Hindu, or the Muslim. I am content to learn from them and to walk with them side by side toward the God who lives, I believe, beyond the images that bind and blind us all." With those words, Spong issued a blanket rejection of the Great Commission Jesus gave to the Church.

What we are seeing today is a redefinition of truth. Some call it the "death of truth." Whereas the Church through the centuries used to talk about *knowing* the truth, *heeding* and *obeying* the truth, we now hear new definitions and understandings. In the new understanding, truth has become the construct of one's group or sub-group. Persons can tell their own story, but it is "true" only for them. There remains no common or universal reference point of truth which is used as a guide. You have your truth; I have mine. In fact, any universal claim to truth is often criticized today because it supposedly excludes other views and even does "violence" to persons by marginalizing their views. Thus, truth today, if it even is mentioned, has become totally subjective. We have created a democracy of ideas, insisting that all ideas are created equal.

As evangelicals, we share John Wesley's belief that many theological issues are worthy of exploration and honestly held differences of opinion. However, we share Wesley's belief that there are essential Christian doctrines that are not up for whimsical debate such as the resurrection of Christ—which cuts at the root of our faith.

The question, then, is this: Can bishops, pastors, and theologians continue mishandling "the word of truth" and retain integrity or credibility? In his essay on "Christian Apologetics," C. S. Lewis says no. Speaking to a group of Anglican priests back in 1945 (I told you this was nothing new), he suggested that if they exceed the boundaries of Anglican and/or Christian doctrine, it was their duty, as an act of personal integrity, to change professions. The issue, he added, was not whether they had come to their unorthodox doctrines honestly. What he denied was that they could receive money and support from the church as priests while at the same time teach and embrace doctrines contrary to the church's teaching.

Lewis became even more clear: "We are to defend Christianity itself—the faith preached by the Apostles, attested by the Martyrs, embodied in the Creeds, expounded by the Fathers. This must be clearly distinguished from the whole of what any one of us may think about God and man. Each of us has his individual emphasis; each holds, in addition to the faith, many opinions which seem to him to be consistent with it and true and important. And so, perhaps, they are. But as apologists it is not our business to defend them. We are defending Christianity, not 'my religion.'"

That sounds like what those North Central Jurisdiction bishops were charged to do at their consecration. And it is what all of us who are ordained elders have promised to do as well.

March/April 2001

TEN

Getting the gospel right

How ironic is it that for several hundred years Christians have defended their faith against attacks of atheists who argued all religions are false? Now we face the opposite extreme that claims all religions are true. Clearly, those aren't the beliefs for which the martyrs suffered and died.

At my annual conference this June (1999), several references were made to the upcoming General Conference. Some predicted a "War on the Shore" as delegates gather from a deeply divided denomination. A greater danger might be that delegates, wishing to have a "positive" experience, might refuse to acknowledge their differences.

It is arguable that United Methodism has two different religions functioning under one large ecclesiastical tent. One would be historic Christianity and the other would be various expressions of liberal teaching mixed with New Age spirituality. We are assured that our deep differences don't really matter. We should all still be able to live under one roof.

It struck me recently how long this condition has existed within United Methodism. I was ordained an elder in 1969. During those 30 years, the revisionist themes have changed very little. They go something like this: The Scriptures are of human origin, not divine; Jesus was not born of a virgin nor was he raised from the dead; Jesus never claimed divinity for himself and was no different than you or I; and humankind is basically good, not sinful; etc. I've heard those themes from United Methodist theologians, read them in our publications, and spoken with distraught church members whose pastors have preached them from their pulpits.

More recently, Professor Marcus Borg has been busy telling us that

Jesus performed no miracles, was merely a mystic and social reformer; that God is not the creator of our universe; that the New Testament stories aren't really true; and that God doesn't care if we are Muslim, Buddhist, or Hindu.

How ironic is it that for several hundred years Christians have defended their faith against attacks of atheists who argued all religions are *false?* Now we face the opposite extreme that claims all religions are *true.* Clearly, those aren't the beliefs for which the martyrs suffered and died.

This context makes all the more timely the arrival of the statement, "The Gospel of Jesus Christ: An Evangelical Celebration," in *Christianity Today* (June 14, 1999). The new statement is the work of a drafting committee of respected evangelicals such as Maxie Dunnam, Timothy George, Thomas Oden, and J. I. Packer.

David Neff, executive editor of *Christianity Today,* writing for the drafting committee, said that in evangelicals' ongoing contact and collaboration with the historic churches, "it is time for us to revisit, reaffirm, and recapture the gospel." He added that as religious bodies and Christian leaders come together to enrich one another and work together, "the biblical understanding of the good news is, first, *the most important thing that we can offer friends in these churches and, second, the only thing in which we can find true unity"* (emphasis mine). Neff noted the infinite capacity of human beings for "getting things wrong," and unfortunately, "we have often gotten the gospel wrong," he writes.

"An Evangelical Celebration" has a refreshing boldness and candor about it. In the Preamble, it states unapologetically, "This gospel is the only gospel; there is no other; and to change its substance is to pervert and indeed destroy it." Little room for "Re-Imagining" there.

The statement is attempting to say, "This is what the good news really is!" Consider, for example, this candid affirmation: "The moment we truly believe in Christ, the Father declares us righteous in him and begins conforming us to his likeness. Genuine faith acknowledges and depends upon Jesus as Lord and shows itself in growing obedience to the divine commands."

Again, we are reminded that "Salvation in its full sense is from the guilt of sin in the past, the power of sin in the present, and the presence of sin in the future." And again, "Salvation is a Trinitarian reality, initiated by the Father, implemented by the Son, and applied by the Holy Spirit." There is a vibrant clarity in these affirmations.

In the tradition of the Barmen Declaration of 50 years ago, "An Evangelical Celebration" concludes with a list of 18 Affirmations and Denials. For example, "*We affirm* that the gospel diagnoses the universal human condition as one of sinful rebellion against God. *We deny* any rejection of the fallenness of human nature or any assertion of the natural goodness, or divinity, of the human race."

Another example: "We affirm that the bodily resurrection of Christ from the dead is essential to the biblical gospel (I Corinthians 15:14). We deny the validity of any so-called gospel that denies the historical reality of the bodily resurrection of Christ." This is refreshingly straightforward.

United Methodists must realize anew that a "biblical understanding of the good news is, first, the most important thing that we can offer." Also, we must confess that for too long, we have "gotten the gospel wrong" and the results of that have been catastrophic. "An Evangelical Celebration" is one of the clearest statements made recently as to the essence of the gospel. It is this gospel, not any other, we are expected to believe and commissioned to proclaim.

September/October 1999

ELEVEN

Practioners for the soul

This is what someone recently called "Designer Christianity." It's a religion fashioned according to one's personal likes and preferences. We're told that if we just design it right, removing the difficult and objectionable parts, this faith will find wide acceptance in today's fickle, secular culture.

Two months ago I was in the hospital for a second angioplasty. I'm still amazed at this delicate procedure. I recall being awake there in the sanitized operating room while several doctors ran a fine wire into my left anterior artery to "balloon" it open and then place another small stainless-steel stent in the artery to help keep it open.

As I think about that procedure, I realize that one thing I want for sure is *precision*. This is no time for a sloppy "hit and miss" procedure. I also want *honesty*. I want a doctor who can say, "I know what needs to be done. I'm properly trained and can do it well." What I don't want is a doctor who says casually, "They taught me angioplasty in medical school, but I have my own theories. I don't like to be confined. I enjoy experimentation." Just the thought is laughable. Not on my arteries you won't!

Sometimes I wonder if that is not how some in the United Methodist Church are approaching the task of Christian ministry, or "the cure of souls," as it used to be called. Many, like Wesley, still want to know "the way to heaven." But many clergy today would respond by beginning a debate about the existence of heaven. Others would speculate about the many and various roads that one can take to get there, all having their own merit. They, too, enjoy "experimentation" and don't want "to be confined." This is what someone recently called "Designer Christianity." It's a religion fashioned according to one's personal likes and preferences. We're told that if we just design it right, removing the difficult and objectionable parts, this faith will find wide acceptance in today's fickle, secular culture.

How many times have we heard about a United Methodist pastor concluding a faithful ministry only to be followed by a pastor who unloads a totally different theology, a different set of moral standards, and a dumpster load of questions about the Bible and its trustworthiness? The result: discouraged parishioners usually scatter to safer pastures in some other church. Others, more patient perhaps (or less theologically grounded), wait charitably for their new pastor to begin making sense.

What's missing? Two things: *precision* and *honesty*.

A chief characteristic of the mainline protestant church for the past three decades has been *ambiguity*. You've heard it often. "We can't really understand the mystery of God." "No one faith statement fully comprehends the Almighty." "No one should claim certainty about matters of faith—holy ambiguity should be our posture." That even sounds humble, doesn't it?

Theologian R. R. Reno observes that ambiguity, unlike clarity or precision, can neither persuade nor even sustain itself on its own. Weak and vague convictions, not strong ones, are more likely to cause oppression since ambiguity needs to be protected, propped up, and promoted by force.

One of the things I have always appreciated about the Lausanne Covenant, an evangelical statement of faith produced at the Lausanne Congress on Evangelism in 1974, is that its statements are clear and precise. Its definition of evangelism is a great example: "*To evangelize is to spread the good news that Jesus Christ died for our sins and was raised from the dead according to the Scriptures, and that as the reigning Lord he now offers the forgiveness of sins and the liberating gift of the Spirit to all who repent and believe.*" That's precision! We expect it from our surgeons. We need it from our clergy.

Lay persons deserve both precision and honesty as well. Gerd Ludemann, currently a New Testament professor at Gottingen University in Germany, had taught at Vanderbilt Divinity School and other protestant seminaries. While teaching, he came to reject all central Christian doctrines one by one. Finally, concluding that Jesus did not rise from the dead and that the biblical account of him was pure fairy tale, he admitted publicly that he could no longer call himself a Christian, because he plainly was not one. Then, having become honest about himself, he turned his attention to church bureaucrats and liberal theologians. In trying to reformulate Christian doctrine into something they can believe, he says many church officials are "interpreting" the words of the creeds into meaninglessness, a process he calls "contemptible." And we would add, dishonest.

Writing in the *Alberta Report* (Canada), Ted and Virginia Byfield asked why these church officials and theologians don't join Ludemann in his honesty, and admit their own unbelief. The reason they don't, said the Byfields, is they are on the church payroll. To announce their actual unbelief would invite them off church payrolls. So, they avoid getting specific in doctrinal matters. "They keep everything blurred, hazy, and inconclusive," wrote the Byfields.

Church officials, whether they are pastors, bureaucrats, or bishops, who do not affirm the doctrines of the Christian faith, should as an act of personal integrity admit they have moved beyond the doctrines of historic Christianity and change vocations. One has the freedom to disavow the major doctrines of Christian faith, but one is not being honest in claiming that the leftovers qualify as being consistent with the classic, historic Christian faith.

July/August 1999

TWELVE

The historicity of our faith

Earlier, theological liberalism tried to excise the supernatural elements out of the biblical text. The historicity of the gospels was replaced with a vague admiration of Jesus as a good teacher and example, but not the risen Lord.

One of the remarkable features of our day is the number of theologians who are in popular demand to tell mainline Christian audiences all the things they no longer believe about historic Christianity. Marcus Borg, a Jesus Seminar Fellow, quickly comes to mind.

Borg was the featured lecturer at Iliff School of Theology's Warren Lectures in January (1999). In February he spoke at the National Conference of Christian Educators Fellowship in Chicago, an ecumenical event which attracted 600 United Methodists.

Borg is not shy in telling his audiences what he no longer believes. In seminary he learned that the stories of the Bible "can be factually true without being literally true." In his lectures at Iliff and in Chicago, Borg renounced his belief in such things as Jesus' virgin birth, the feeding of the 5,000, and Jesus' walking on the water, amongst other things.

According to Borg, Jesus never claimed divinity for himself or believed that his death would be a sacrifice for the sins of the world. His belief that the resurrection did not happen follows naturally. For Borg, Jesus was a Jewish prophet and mystic, who died a martyr's death because he opposed the power structures of his day.

One might dismiss all this as minimally important, but Borg has appeared as a "cutting edge" theologian before seminarians who will one day fill our United Methodist pulpits and before Christian educators who are already on the job.

Furthermore, United Methodist Bishop Joe Sprague (since

retired) not only warmly reviewed Borg's writings, but also planned to send a copy of Borg's latest book to every pastor in the Northern Illinois Conference to be the focus of a study day on the district. (The publisher failed to send the books and a January snowstorm cancelled the day on the district.) So, we should not dismiss Borg's popularity lightly.

Several things need to be said. First, the Jesus Seminar is a self-selected group of scholars who meet periodically to cast votes on what they think Jesus actually said and did (using color-coded cards to vote). The group has received far more press coverage than its scholarship merits.

Dr. Luke Timothy Johnson, professor of New Testament and Christian origins at the Candler School of Theology at Emory University, has been one of many outspoken critics of the Jesus Seminar and its faulty scholarship. Johnson contends that the selection of the seminar members was based not on quality of scholarship but on prior agreement to discover a particular "Jesus"—that is, one who fits the "countercultural attitude favored by liberal academics." Johnson was quoted in *Time* magazine a few years ago referring to the Seminar as a "ten-year exercise in academic self-promotion" whose bias generates "bad history and bad theology."

Second, to question the historicity of the Christian faith is nothing new. To borrow a phrase, we are "meeting liberalism again for the first time." Early in this century, theological liberalism tried to excise the supernatural elements out of the biblical text. The historicity of the gospels was replaced with a vague admiration of Jesus as a good teacher and example, but not the risen Lord.

J. Gresham Machen responded to this trend in 1921 with an address which was printed in *The Princeton Theological Review* and then published in 1923 as his classic *Christianity and Liberalism*. In it Machen charged, "'Christ died for our sins'...From the beginning, the Christian gospel...consisted in an account of something that had happened. And from the beginning, the meaning of the happening was set forth; and when the meaning of the happening was set forth then there was Christian doctrine. 'Christ died'—that is history; 'Christ died for our sins'—that is doctrine. Without these two elements, joined in an absolutely indissoluble union, there is no Christianity." To eliminate the historicity of Christianity is to be left with something that is not historic Christian faith.

United Methodist pastor, J. Keith Goodlett, in his excellent work *Window To The World*, rightly observes that one of the popular strategies to disprove or cast doubt on the substance of the biblical message is to simply undermine the Bible's historical reliability, which is actually its foundation. Goodlett, an elder in the South Georgia Conference, reminds us that "Christianity is dependent upon literal history. The creeds of the early church are affirmations of belief in the actuality of a number of historical events."

This debate is not just academic exercise, nor are these distinctions inconsequential. They get at the core of our faith. Last Sunday our chancel choir performance of "The Seven Last Words of Christ" moved many of us to tears and renewed devotion. I thought of Borg's denials as I listened. Was it *really* Christ Jesus? Did he *actually speak* those words to the ages? My eyes then fell upon a hymn Charles Wesley wrote in 1742, and I wept as I read: "*O Love divine, what hast thou done! The immortal God hath died for me! The Father's co-eternal Son bore all my sins upon the tree. Th' immortal God for me hath died: My Lord, my Love, is crucified!*"

If one believes Borg, one must dismiss Charles Wesley. For they are espousing two different religions.

May/June 1999

Part 2
TRUTH AND CHURCH UNITY

THIRTEEN

The gospel of radical inclusion

"This [theology of radical inclusion] isn't an ethical divide.... It's a theological chasm — one that separates those who hold a theology of divine acceptance from those who hold a theology of divine redemption."

The mainline Protestant Church in America suffers today from a dogmatic indifference to truth. The so-called progressives would define this indifference as tolerance and say it is good. Above all, we dare not be judgmental or exclusive.

Throughout more than 35 years of ministry, I have witnessed this indifference expressed in various ways. For example: God is so vast as to be beyond our comprehension. Or, the Divine is an ineffable mystery that none of us can fully understand. Or, as St. Paul said, "We see through a glass dimly." This is the same Paul, by the way, who authored Romans; who twice said to the Galatians, "If anybody is preaching to you a gospel other than what you accepted, let him be eternally condemned!" (Galatians 1:9).

This passage came to mind when I first read Philip Turner's article, "An Unworkable Theology," in *First Things*. It struck me as profoundly relevant, not only for the Episcopal Church USA, but for United Methodists as well.

Turner is the former Dean of Berkeley Divinity School at Yale. He notes at the outset that mainline Protestantism is in a state of disintegration. While attendance declines and internal divisions increase, the Episcopal Church's problem, he writes, "is far more theological than it is moral—a theological poverty that is truly monumental and that stands behind the moral missteps recently taken by its governing bodies." (He's referring to his church's election and consecration as bishop of the Rev. V. Gene Robinson, a practicing homosexual.)

What is this theological poverty he writes about? It is a reduction of the Christian gospel to a shallow, simplistic message that "God is love. God loves us. We, therefore, ought to love one another." What's been missing in Episcopal sermons for years, he notes, is any mention of Christ's death seen as judgment on the human condition, no mention of resurrection, of the promised Holy Spirit, or repentance and holiness of life.

From the simplistic affirmation "God is love" comes a further point, he says. "That accepting love requires a form of justice that is inclusive of all people, particularly those who in some way have been marginalized by oppressive social practice. The mission of the Church is, therefore, to see that those who have been rejected are included.... The result is a practical equivalence between the gospel of the Kingdom of God and a particular form of social justice." In other words, you have the equation of the gospel with social justice, defined as radical inclusion or, as some would say, "diversity."

All of this becomes vitally important for Turner when the church discusses matters such as homosexual practice and same-sex marriage. He writes, "This isn't an ethical divide.... It's a theological chasm—one that separates those who hold a theology of divine *acceptance* from those who hold a theology of divine *redemption*."

This is the critical distinction that defines the different understandings about how the church today should be in ministry with persons practicing homosexuality. Scripturally-oriented ministries work with persons lovingly with the hope of transformation and redemption. Progressives, on the other hand, view ministry as lovingly affirming persons as they are, as God has supposedly "created them." Transformation or redemption are not sought so much as self-actualization and affirmation. These are serious differences.

As for United Methodists, in light of the loss of another 80,000 members last year, and more than three million since the merger in 1968, it is time we ask whether we are getting the gospel right. Is radical inclusion a good summary of the gospel? All of us would affirm that biblical inclusivism has helped the church overcome racial, gender, and other boundaries that needed removed. But inclusivism has become an ideology today used in the exercise of raw power (see William J. Abraham, "Inclusivism, Idolatry and the Survival of the (Fittest) Faithful," *The Community of the Word*). We have even been told "that to embrace diversity is to embrace God."

Dr. Dan Church, former head of our General Council on Ministries, addressed this problem before the Council of Bishops in 2001: "Some say we have made a God of diversity. They say that, whereas 'inclusivity' should be a symptom of our godliness, the 'fruit,' if you will, we have made inclusivity our God. It doesn't matter what you believe, they say, it only matters that everyone is at the table."

Turner warns, "In a theology dominated by radical inclusion, terms such as 'faith,' 'justification,' 'repentance,' and 'holiness of life' seem to belong to an antique vocabulary that must be outgrown or reinterpreted."

The working theology of the Episcopal Church, he concludes, is one "which most Anglicans in the rest of the world no longer recognize as Christian." How about the working theology of us United Methodists?

July/August 2006

FOURTEEN

Unity and mainline churches

The common thread found in all of the revisionists, who would suddenly—after two millennia of Christian teaching—bring to the church a radical new understanding of sexuality, marriage, and family, is that the Scriptures are no longer authoritative or relevant when discussing human sexuality.

For 25 years, I have been meeting annually with renewal leaders from the mainline denominations in the United States. In 1996, we gave this fellowship a name—the Association for Church Renewal. Participants include leaders from renewal ministries in all of the mainline denominations in North America, including the United Church of Canada.

What this group has discovered is that all of the mainline/oldline churches have been struggling for more than two decades with identical problems: membership loss, decay of Scriptural authority, doctrinal defection, pro-homosexual activism, and the embracing of trendy, new theologies. None of them report any real sense of unity in their denominations.

To the contrary, several of the mainline churches are struggling to hold together, being pushed to the brink of division by pro-homosexual activists.

For example, the Episcopal Church USA (ECUSA) has a new evangelical network which came into existence in January of 2004—The Network of Anglican Communion Dioceses and Parishes. The new network represents thousands of laity and clergy within ECUSA who refuse to accept the consecration as bishop in November 2003 of V. Gene Robinson, a self-acknowledged homosexual priest. Within just one week of its founding, the Network had been recognized by 14 Anglican archbishops who represent a majority of the 75-million, world-wide Anglican Communion. In addition, a number of archbishops have broken Communion fellowship with the ECUSA.

More recently, the four-million member Presbyterian Church of East Africa (PCEA) served notice to the Presbyterian Church USA that it will not continue fellowship with any regional presbytery or church that supports homosexuality. So, the unwillingness of PCUSA leaders to enforce their own constitutional prohibition against the ordination of practicing homosexuals has begun to have global consequences.

The Presbyterian Church of East Africa ordered one of its presbyteries to discontinue immediately its partnership with the National Capital Presbytery in Washington, D.C. National Capital is one of the presbyteries that is supportive of homosexual ordination of Presbyterian clergy.

The East Africa Presbyterian body receives about $300,000 a year from PCUSA churches, so its courageous action could mean a loss of funds. However, PCEA general secretary Samuel Muriguh said, "The idea of lesbianism or gay-ism is unbiblical. We have our integrity to uphold. It is better to go without the money."

Renewal leaders in the 5.2-million Evangelical Lutheran Church in America report the possibility of division in 2005 when a task force studying homosexuality and same-sex unions makes its report to that denomination's major legislative body.

And finally, of course, delegates at the 2004 United Methodist General Conference in Pittsburgh hurriedly passed a resolution on the final day of conference affirming a unity that everyone knows is non-existent.

The common thread found in all of the revisionists, who would suddenly—after two millennia of Christian teaching—bring to the church a radical new understanding of sexuality, marriage, and family, is that Scripture is no longer authoritative or relevant when discussing human sexuality. They hold that the Scriptures must be trumped by new learning and new understanding.

Writing in his chapter in *Staying the Course*, Dr. William J. Abraham says: "The enduring strength of drawing on Scripture in the Christian church is that it is essentially an appeal to special revelation." By appeal to reason and experience, says Abraham, we only know partially who we are, what our nature is, and how we are supposed to live. He goes on to say, "Reason and experience, though important and even indispensable, are insufficient and inadequate. We depend substantially and nontrivially on divine revelation."

Here is where we get to the heart of the differences that are dividing the mainline churches today. Is the church dealing with an authoritative divine revelation that is normative for its life and work today? Or are there new normative sources to guide and inform the church, which are coming to us from sources *other than* Scripture? Does God reveal his will to us through human experience and cultural change, or through Scripture as divine revelation?

Richard John Neuhaus answers these questions well. "Christianity is not based upon experience, reason, or our inherited wisdom, but upon God's self-disclosure in history. Christian thinking, whether about God, about Christ, about moral life, or culture must always begin with what has been made known." We begin with God's "special revelation" of Scripture.

Churches will never experience unity if the divine revelation of Scripture is set aside for a more contemporary norm for its teaching and preaching.

July/August 2004

FIFTEEN

A bittersweet 2004 General Conference

The chair's welcome of the demonstrators
(without asking the body for permission),
the placement of a rainbow-colored candle in the
worship area, and expressions of support from more
than 25 bishops (both active and retired),
who stood in solidarity with the protesters,
combined to leave many of us with a
sinking feeling in the pits of our stomachs.

The 2004 General Conference in Pittsburgh has come and gone. All of us continue to examine actions taken and their significance. We hope this special General Conference issue of GOOD NEWS will help United Methodists have a better understanding about what happened there.

On many of the cultural issues facing the church, the momentum from General Conference 2000 in Cleveland continued. Unfortunately, the last several General Conferences have evolved into two-week battles over homosexuality. The reason that *The New York Times* sends a reporter is to cover our debates regarding sexuality, not because we have a new evangelism emphasis or social action initiative.

Having said that, we are grateful for the votes on marriage and sexuality: delegates affirmed and even strengthened the prohibition against the ordination and appointment of self-avowed, practicing homosexuals by a 73 percent vote; a motion to allow gay marriages was defeated by an 83 percent vote and performing one was added to the *Discipline* as a "chargeable offense;" a motion to require the Boy Scouts to include homosexuals was defeated by a strong 80 percent vote.

Delegates voted to "support laws in civil society that define marriage as the union of one man and one woman," by a 77 percent majority vote. We are the first and only mainline church to be on record on this issue.

These and other actions by delegates reflect a church that is moving away from, not toward, libertarian sexual ethics. The momentum here is toward strengthening biblical values.

The Judicial Council made two very important rulings while in Pittsburgh. The first clarified that our church stance prohibiting self-avowed practicing homosexuals from ordination and appointment is, in fact, church law. The second ruling, while not overturning the egregious Karen Dammann trial verdict, ruled that no pastor found by a trial court to be a self-avowed practicing homosexual can be appointed in the UM Church. (This ruling may be part of the reason Dammann has decided not to seek appointment this spring.) Also, newly elected members to the Judicial Council make us confident it will continue to uphold and faithfully interpret the *Book of Discipline*.

Another positive action by delegates in Pittsburgh was the vote to change the representation on our church's boards and agencies so they reflect more fairly our regional membership numbers. This means, simply, that the growing, more traditional Southeastern, South Central, and Central Conferences will have more persons on program boards and agencies.

Despite these many positive legislative actions (and some not so positive—no judicial review or Women's Division reform legislation got passed), many of us returned home feeling anything but victorious.

We recall a shattered communion chalice that was broken by a pro-gay activist after delegates voted to retain our stance on homosexuality. (I've yet to see *any* media account critical of that rude, intemperate act.) Then, two days later we endured the 35-minute protest orchestrated by Soulforce, a gay-rights organization, which had unhindered access to the floor of General Conference. The chair's welcome of the demonstrators (without asking the body for permission), the placement of a rainbow-colored candle in the worship area, and expressions of support from more than 25 bishops (both active and retired), who stood in solidarity with the protesters, combined to leave many of us with a sinking feeling in the pits of our stomachs. These were not holy moments. Candles, baptismal water, and chalices are meant for worship, not political theater.

The 2004 General Conference will be remembered as the one at which the subject of amicable separation was placed on the table for United Methodists to discuss. We must listen prayerfully to discern what the Spirit is saying to the church about this. But continued defiance of the *Book of Discipline* and repeated declarations by "progressives" (and for that matter the entire Western Jurisdiction) that they plan to ignore the church's standards, leave us asking if there is not a better way forward. (In Washington State, one of our churches recently lost 60 *families* (!) over the homosexuality controversy.)

Good News affirms the goal of unity in the church. However, it should be very clear that the unity resolution passed at General Conference was little more than window dressing. How ironic it was to have delegates holding hands across that massive convention center and to be led in singing "Blest Be the Tie that Binds" by Bishop Joe Sprague—the most controversial and theologically divisive bishop in recent UM history. Despite the unity resolution, we are not a united church.

Our unity will come only from faithful adherence to the Apostolic faith. That faith centers on historical events (the birth, life, death, resurrection, ascension of Jesus, and the giving of the Holy Spirit) and on the historical, trustworthy testimony by eyewitnesses provided for us in Holy Scripture. It is this scriptural foundation alone, made alive by the Spirit's presence among us, that will save the United Methodist Church from ungrounded subjectivism, doctrinal revisionism, and continued spiritual deterioration.

May/June 2004

SIXTEEN

The affectation of unity

Why is this affectation of unity so scandalous?
Because, writes Professor Robert George, "It tends
to damage and weaken the faith of those who are
exposed to it. It sends a message to them that the
core doctrines and moral teachings of Christianity
need not be taken too seriously."

Division in the body of Christ is a scandal. Most all agree with that. We must never be satisfied or content with it, as we work and pray for unity. But evangelicals have always held something as more important than Christian unity—faithfulness to apostolic doctrines and moral teachings.

Unfortunately, most talk we hear about unity has been unity-at-any-price, which ultimately means unity at the cost of biblical truth. E. J. Carnell voiced concern about this many years ago, noting the disturbing openness of the ecumenical movement at the time. It would readily welcome those who were open antagonists to major doctrines such as the resurrection, which led him to charge, "Whether Christ conquered death is apparently not important. The important thing is that we all get together under one roof."

In a recent issue of *Touchstone* journal, Professor Robert George of Princeton University wrote that there is something even worse than the scandal of division in the Church. It is the scandal of the "affectation of unity between those who do and those who do not affirm the core doctrines of Christian faith—particularly its most fundamental moral teachings."

What is an "affectation of unity?" An affectation is a "pretending, a pretense, an artificial behavior meant to impress others." So an affectation of unity is a pretending to be united, a pretense of unity, or a claim to unity that is really artificial, made simply for the sake of others watching. So, the scandal greater than division in the church, says George, is a false unity between "those who do and those who do not affirm the core doctrines of Christian faith."

Why is this affectation of unity so scandalous? Because, writes George, "It tends to damage and weaken the faith of those who are exposed to it. It sends a message to them that the core doctrines and moral teachings of Christianity need not be taken too seriously." It implies to those watching that one can be a "good Christian" while at the same time "disbelieving the doctrines of the Trinity and incarnation, the virgin birth and bodily resurrection of Jesus...." When it comes to such serious matters, "we encounter divisions that must be sustained. There is no core of common faith on which to build," he writes.

As I read Professor George's discussion, I was reminded of Harold Paul Sloan, a prominent Methodist pastor in the New Jersey Conference, who led a grassroots effort in the 1920s. Sloan founded the Methodist League for Faith and Life, a movement whose purpose was to "meet this Modernist current and drive which is threatening Methodism." This was the era when theological liberalism was devastating the American church.

At the 1928 General Conference, Sloan delivered a petition with 10,000 signatures from 522 Methodist churches in 41 states! He charged Methodist seminaries, pulpits, and literature with serious disloyalty to Methodist doctrinal standards. It was a major expression from across the denomination. Delegates, however, refused to give heed to his concerns.

There is more about Sloan's effort. I found it in retired Bishop William B. Lewis' unpublished doctoral thesis on Sloan some time ago. In 1926, Bishop Adna W. Leonard became a friend of Sloan. Leonard, in fact, was positive about, and in agreement with, Sloan's Methodist League. Soon, Bishop Leonard met with Sloan, another bishop, and others at Wannamaker's in Philadelphia to discuss plans to help advance the cause of the Methodist League. The very next month, Bishop Leonard visited Sloan in his Haddonfield home and helped him lay plans for League strategy. Throughout the rest of the year, Bishop Leonard was constant in his advice and support of Sloan and the League.

By January, 1927, Bishop Leonard was prepared to write an article to launch the newly-named publication of the League, *The Essentialist.* Just weeks before the deadline, Sloan got the devastating news. Bishop Leonard said in a letter to Sloan, "In view of all the matters involved, I feel under the necessity of saying that it will not be possible for me to identify myself with The League for Faith and Life as one of its members." In a letter to the New York *Christian Advocate*, Leonard denied any association with the League.

Sloan was crushed but kept the matter in close confidence. The Methodist Board of Bishops continued to present a united front in its relationship to the Modernist controversy within the church, even though many bishops were distressed by the church's theological unfaithfulness. When faced with the choice between unity and truth, the Methodist Board of Bishops wrongly chose unity.

Harold Paul Sloan, however, having spoken intimately and often with Leonard and other bishops about Methodism's theological defections, knew well that the bishops were presenting to the church "an affectation of unity."

Robert George is right. The affectation of unity is the greater scandal.

November/December 2003

SEVENTEEN

The risk of renewal groups

"Our denomination is at great risk. The time to act is now. Organizations calling themselves 'conservative renewal groups' are engaged in campaigns to change the essential nature of our church," the authors claim. "They seek to take the church to a place where diversity and tolerance and breadth of spirit are in short supply."

Every so often, something happens to illustrate the widening doctrinal chasm that still exists within the United Methodist Church. Perhaps the most recent example of this divide is the recent publication of *United Methodism @ Risk: A Wake-Up Call*. The book is an attack on all the United Methodist evangelical renewal ministries, including of course, Good News. Because of these various evangelical groups, the church is supposedly somehow "at risk."

The book comes from the Information Project for United Methodists, an ad hoc group of liberal leaders and long-time church activists. Retired Bishop Dale White heads the project. Others involved include well-known names such as Bishop Roy Sano, Ms. Peggy Billings, the Rev. Jeanne Audrey Powers, and Dr. Tex Sample.

One can't help but smile at the hyperventilated sense of alarm found in the opening sentences of the book's preface, "Our denomination is at great risk. The time to act is now. Organizations calling themselves 'conservative renewal groups' are engaged in campaigns to change the essential nature of our church. They seek to take the church to a place where diversity and tolerance and breadth of spirit are in short supply."

Readers should not miss the irony here. While espousing the virtue of tolerance, here is a book which is *utterly intolerant of all the*

UM evangelical renewal groups.

Though it was produced by a bishop, an attorney, and a "skilled research team" who labored months on the effort, the book is laced with numerous errors. Admittedly, we all might do renewal ministry better. None of us would claim we have always said it and done it right. But these liberal critics have an embarrassingly limited understanding of the church's evangelical groups. They really don't seem to know us at all. Consider a few examples:

• The book has me "at the helm" of the Confessing Movement, which has *never* been the case. The Confessing Movement is a totally different ministry than Good News, with a different board of directors. That ministry was launched by a gathering of evangelicals called by Bishop William Cannon, Dr. Thomas C. Oden, and Dr. Maxie Dunnam. Sen. Pat Miller soon became (and remains) the executive director of that movement. Even the most simple inquiry about our two groups would have revealed they are separate.

• In the paragraph dealing with the Houston Declaration of 1988, the book claims the Declaration's authors were "Good News leaders." Wrong again. Those responsible for the Houston Declaration included the Revs. Bill Hinson, Maxie Dunnam, Ellsworth Kalas, Jimmy Buskirk, Ira Gallaway, John Ed Mathison, and Gerald Trigg. None of these were "Good News leaders."

• In the book's comments about the Mission Society for United Methodists, the author says "but nothing in the Mission Society's public material suggests a holistic view of mission. It's about Americans going overseas." This embarrassingly uninformed statement reveals these critics know virtually nothing about the impressive, holistic ministry of the Mission Society, which is now in its 19th year of operation with 153 missionaries on the field. [At the time of editing this for publication, it is now in its 22nd year with 180 missionaries on the field.] The critics just know it involves evangelicals and/or conservatives, and thus they are against it.

The book is critical of Good News for seeking "to mandate fidelity on the part of clergy" to what we call "classical Christianity." To that, we admit we are guilty as charged. We believe pastors should be faithful to the church's doctrinal standards. And so, we would add, does *The Book of Discipline.* And so too, it would seem, do Boards of Ordained Ministry.

At the heart of this book's disagreement with evangelicals is the role of doctrine in our church. We are not, says this book, a creedal or confessional church. We don't use doctrine "as an instrument of inquisition." (Readers with any sense of fairness will recognize that latter statement as a grossly unfair stereotype of all Christians who take theology seriously.)

The book claims, rather, that we Methodists have "reached across significant theological disagreements to declare to one another Wesley's words: 'If your heart be as my heart, then give me your hand.'" This notoriously misquoted phrase, of course, comes from Wesley's sermon, "Catholic Spirit." The phrase is the popular trump card played so often to justify our long neglect of theology. "If your heart is somehow warm like mine is, then let's just shake hands and not worry about doctrine."

But what did Wesley mean by the heart and hand quotation? Much more than most think. He spends no less than seven lengthy paragraphs explaining it. He asks: "Do you believe...?, Do you believe...?, Have you the divine evidence...?" Clearly, for Wesley, right doctrine—including Christ's deity and atoning death—was a vital ingredient for a right heart. Wesley would never extend a conciliatory hand to one who denied the authority of Scripture or the deity of Jesus Christ, as if those doctrines didn't matter. Wesley even goes on to describe "this unsettledness of thought," "this being...'tossed about with every wind of doctrine,'" as "a great curse, not a blessing." He then says boldly: "A man of a truly catholic spirit has not now his religion to seek. He is fixed as the sun in his judgment concerning the main branches of Christian doctrine."

For those of us involved in evangelical renewal, we believe what really is @ risk today is our Wesleyan doctrinal heritage.

July/August 2003

EIGHTEEN

The ties that bind

For more than 35 years, Good News has been openly at work within the United Methodist Church as a catalyst for theological and spiritual renewal. Some folks may not agree with every stand that we take, for sure. But it is sad to see the not-so-subtle hint that we should be passive and quiet in the back of the bus lest we get kicked off.

When the Supervisory Response Team announced it was dismissing the charges against Bishop Joe Sprague, the statement acknowledged there was room for both dissent and reform in the Church. It went on to plead that the various groups conduct this discourse "without personal attack."

That is, for sure, an appropriate statement. That's why a paid advertisement that ran in the *UMConnection*, the official paper of the Baltimore-Washington Annual Conference, caught our attention. A group of sixteen retired clergy and laity in that area (including well-known names such as Dr. Phil Wogaman, Bishop Forrest Stith (retired), the Rev. William Holmes, and Mr. Harry Kiely) used the ad to make an unusually severe and unsettling attack on Good News.

The ad noted that General Conferences in the past had shown hospitality to "diverse caucuses and special interests to promote their points of view." However, there is one caucus that concerns them and that is Good News. They feel we have worn out our welcome (they seem to view themselves as the gatekeepers of United Methodist hospitality).

While admitting the denomination can profit from hearing "genuinely committed voices pressing us on what constitutes biblical, Wesleyan, and evangelical imperatives," they charge: "But when any group claims for itself the exclusive custody of 'Scriptural Christianity,' sole guardianship of Wesleyan theology, and infallible interpretation of what constitutes 'Good News,' that group not only violates Wesley's own collegial spirit toward other Christians, but also exploits the hospitality upon which its very presence depends."

What is not presented is a single notation or quote as to where Good News has *ever* claimed exclusive custody, sole guardianship, or infallible interpretation of anything. Since the beginning, Good News has been "A Forum for Scriptural Christianity," not "*The* Forum." We have called ourselves "*a* voice for renewal," not "*the* voice."

Surprisingly, the group drags out once again a 15 year old accusation that Good News is somehow plotting to create an "alternative denomination." Good News, of course, has said from the start that it is a movement for renewal *within* the UM Church. The fact is that many United Methodist evangelicals have elected to remain within the denomination because of hope they find from Good News' ministry.

The specific charges levied against Good News in the advertisement ought to be an embarrassment for those whose names are attached. Consider the following:

• Good News allegedly "has repudiated our Board of Global Ministries by funding and sending forth its own missionaries through a 'shadow' organization they call 'The Mission Society for United Methodists.'" The Mission Society is not a "shadow" anything, of course. It is a supplemental sending agency for United Methodists that has been in existence for 19 years. It has 140 missionaries on the field in more than 30 countries. It has its own board and staff, with headquarters in Norcross, Georgia.

• "Bristol Brooks [surely this spelling is simply a typo] is their alternative to our Abingdon Press," they charge. Well, Good News did launch Bristol Books back in 1989. We were seeking to provide more scriptural and evangelical resources for United Methodists desirous of them. We sold it in 1991, when it became Bristol House, Ltd., a for-profit corporation. In the last few years, Bristol House has worked in cooperation with the United Methodist Publishing House (including Abingdon) on several projects. This includes *Faith Files*, a children's mid-week program, as well as a joint adult study program.

• "Light and Life Press offers church school literature in direct competition with our General Board of Discipleship," the critics charge. This is, again, not right. Light and Life Press is the publishing house for the Free Methodist Church. Bristol House has developed a line of church school curriculum that is solidly Scriptural and Wesleyan in substance, but Light and Life Press has had nothing to do with it.

• "Good News has its own literature for confirmation classes, youth groups, and United Methodist Women," the ad says. The popular *We Believe* confirmation curriculum for youth and adults was first published by Good News in 1976 and is now owned and marketed by Bristol House and is still selling well. It and other of Bristol House's publications can be purchased through the UM Publishing House. (It appears that United Methodist "diversity" and "inclusivity" don't always apply when it comes to evangelical matters.)

For more than 35 years, Good News has been openly at work within the United Methodist Church as a catalyst for theological and spiritual renewal. Some folks may not agree with every stand that we take, for sure. But it is sad to see the not-so-subtle hint that we should be passive and quiet in the back of the bus lest we get kicked off.

There is a new ecumenism around the globe that appreciates authentic Christian diversity. This is very different from the passing parochialism represented in the above ad. Sadly, it reflects the new fundamentalism and intolerance of the left. It whiffs of an old-guard, authoritarian liberalism that once was dominant across the church. Its sad legacy was to give United Methodism 30 consecutive years of membership decline and demoralization. Thankfully, a new era is emerging with the next generation of United Methodists.

May/June 2003

NINETEEN

Dealing with our differences

The strangest thing the Rev. Charles Schuster has seen in the UM Church "is what is now occurring with the Confessing Movement," he writes. "It is seeking a 'creedal' approach to ministry in a denomination 'that has historically been free of such nonsense. Their initiatives are dangerous...'"

We United Methodists struggle with our deep differences. I was reminded of this while reading a recent issue of *Zion's Herald*, a new journal for United Methodists published six times a year by the Boston Wesleyan Association. (While liberal in content, editor Stephen Swecker says he seeks a "broad hospitality" in the magazine. As of January 2007, it will be published as *The Progressive Christian*.)

The current issue carried three articles that provide instructive glimpses as to how United Methodists will be dealing with their differences between now and the 2004 General Conference.

In a brief article, layman Jim Lane of Sherwood, Arkansas, spoke personally about his distress over the ongoing "holy war" in the church. At General Conference last year (Cleveland in 2000), the talk about possible demonstrations, folks being bussed in, and planned disruptions, all left Jim feeling as if there were "a dark cloud hanging over me and the General Conference."

Lane and his wife left Cleveland early after he experienced pains in his left arm and chest. A visit to his doctor back in Arkansas revealed, fortunately, no blocked arteries or heart trouble. The primary cause of his symptoms was stress, his doctor said.

To a colleague who suggested that the issues were, at least, worthy of a fight, Lane replied: "As I get older and hopefully wiser I am even growing weary of that 'good fight'"!

Lane describes battle fatigue. Many of us have felt it. Athanasius must have as well in his 56-year struggle to clarify for the Church that Jesus was fully God and fully man. We must take care not to grow weary in well doing.

In a second article, adapted from his sermon celebrating the anniversary of his church becoming a Reconciling Congregation, the Rev. Robert L. Plaisted writes about the church's need for reconciliation. He says a "Great Divide" exists between liberals and conservatives. Reconciliation is not consensus, we are told, for consensus "requires compromise and eventually agreement." But reconciliation "requires the willingness to live together in peace even when no agreement is possible." Plaisted concludes that we will have to decide whether "we want to win an argument, or do we want to win the world?" We can't do both, he adds. His implication: If the church struggles with important moral concerns such as human sexuality, abortion, pornography, etc., that will keep it from winning the world.

His approach to our differences is to say, "Let's just agree to live together without controversy, even when no agreement is possible." Or, in the words of Richard John Neuhaus, it would be saying that our deepest differences really make no difference. However, this view would leave the church unresistant and undiscerning amidst questionable moral or doctrinal trends, resulting in the church's wholesale accomodation to them.

In a third article, the Rev. Charles Schuster confesses he is "a leg-biting, aggressive, outspoken, obnoxious, obtuse, irritating liberal." When he wakes up in the morning he looks "for a Christian fundamentalist to hassle." Schuster, prominent pastor of Arvada UM Church in Arvada, Colorado, writes about the "strange" things he's seen in his ministry, like a dead snake placed under the hood of a piano causing the pianist to faint, and church trustees who sold manure to help pay for a new parsonage roof. But, he continues, perhaps the strangest thing he has seen in the UM Church "is what is now occurring with the Confessing Movement." It is seeking a "creedal" approach to ministry in a denomination "that has historically been free of such nonsense. Their initiatives are dangerous..." So there they are. A dead snake, a load of manure, and the Confessing Movement— the strange things he has seen in his ministry.

What's going on here? Schuster's approach is to paint evangelicals and their views with the brush of extreme caricature. It's the classic *reductio ad absurdum*, a reducing to the absurd the views and convictions of an opposing group. He likens evangelicals to "hate groups" who have always found ways "of spinning biblical texts so as to condemn those who do not conform to the most recent bigotry. Once it was race, and now it is sexual orientation or creedal compliance." He does have a way with words.

So here are three approaches we hope United Methodists won't use as they grapple with differences in their church—resignation from fatigue, reconciliation at any cost, and ridicule and misrepresentation of orthodox Christian views. If they prevail, it will only deepen the church's present accommodation to the prevailing cultural norms of the day. That is too great a cost for a feigned unity.

July/August 2001

TWENTY

Evangelicals to WCC: Come home

The WCC was launched with the hope that the 147 member denominations present at its founding would be more effective and unified in the task of world missions. Not all present at Amsterdam in 1948 shared that missionary passion.

By the time you read this, the Eighth Assembly of the World Council of Churches (WCC) will be history. The world-wide ecumenical body met in Harare, Zimbabwe, December 3-14, 1998.

What's different about this Assembly is that a team of six evangelicals went as part of an effort by North American evangelicals to call the WCC back to its founding principles. This initiative for WCC reform came from the Association for Church Renewal (ACR), a group of renewal movement executives from the mainline denominations in North America. (I have chaired this group since its founding in October of 1996.)

United Methodist theologian, Thomas Oden, who led the ACR team, said in a news conference at which the initiative was publicly launched, "This could be the last assembly of the World Council of Churches." He noted that the Orthodox member communions were in the process of withdrawal from the WCC. They sent only a low-level delegation to Zimbabwe and chose not to vote. He also added, "Under a rhetoric of inclusiveness, evangelicals have been systematically excluded." In light of the world-wide movement of the Holy Spirit taking place today, the WCC must acknowledge this and become open to evangelical voices and concerns. If not, it will become utterly irrelevant.

The ACR team went to Zimbabwe to try to encourage and network with evangelical delegates from the two-thirds world. The potential for such an effort was seen at last summer's Anglican Bishops' Lambeth

Conference where African and Asian bishops joined with American and British evangelicals to help adopt soundly (by a whopping 526-70 vote) a strong biblical statement on the family and human sexuality.

The ACR initiative also raised a Macedonian call to the leaders of the two-thirds world churches to speak out boldly and prophetically to the churches of the West, which are confused and declining from their acutely impaired moral and theological vision.

The ACR's "Jubilee Appeal" urged the WCC to reject "macro-ecumenism," which would open the ecumenical movement to non-Christian religions. Instead, the evangelicals called the WCC back to its own constitutional definition, which states that the WCC is "a fellowship of churches which confess the Lord Jesus Christ as God and Savior according to the Scriptures and therefore seek to fulfill together their common calling to the glory of the one God, Father, Son, and Holy Spirit." An authentic re-centering of the WCC around this affirmation would revitalize the movement and turn it toward the evangelistic imperative that inspired its founders.

That imperative can be seen in the writing of the late Anglican Bishop Stephen Neill, a respected theologian and one-time associate general secretary of the WCC. He wrote a book in preparation for the Amsterdam Assembly that brought the WCC into being in 1948. In *The Church's Witness to God's Design*, he said, "If an ecumenical movement is not primarily a strategy of worldwide evangelism, then it is nothing but an interesting academic exercise."

The WCC was launched with the hope that the 147-member denominations present at its founding would be more effective and unified in the task of world missions. Not all present at Amsterdam in 1948 shared that missionary passion. Ernest Hocking's famous Layman's Report on Missions expressed the view of many liberal ecumenists of that day. It decried efforts to convert the heathen, claiming the aim of missions was not to convert Buddhists to Christianity but to make Buddhists better Buddhists.

Some 20 years ago, Kenneth Kantzer and Gilbert Beers wrote a joint editorial in *Christianity Today* taking a fresh look at the WCC. They noted several areas of continued concern: 1) The deity of Christ was left undefined and thus only given lip service; 2) The substance of the New Testament Gospel had become lost; 3) The Bible was an honored book from which proof texts were selected, but there was no real Scriptural authority; and 4) Universalism—the view that all will be saved.

In 1973, the WCC conference in Bangkok called for a "moratorium" on crosscultural missionary activity, meaning there should be an indefinite suspension of sending missionaries. For Anglican theologian J.I. Packer, that ended his involvement in the WCC. In *Christianity Today*, he wrote concerning the moratorium, "Was the WCC assuming that universalism is true, so that all will be saved whether evangelized or not? Apparently so." Packer concluded that the new view of Christian world mission "equated present salvation with socio-politico-economic well-being.... The WCC leadership celebrated Bangkok as the close of the era of missions...."

If the WCC does not soon recover its identity as a thoroughly Christian body, it will continue to decline in morale, financial support, and member participation. And well it should. There is no reason for the WCC to lend legitimacy to erring church leaders whose revisionism, deconstruction, and syncretism have helped rob the Christian Church of its uniqueness and its world-wide missionary mandate.

January/February 1999

TWENTY-ONE

In search of unity

"This era's fighting is not about six or seven verses on homosexuality. It's about dozens and dozens of verses on marriage and the order of creation. It is time," said one openly gay UM pastor, "for the left to be more honest. It all has to go. It all has to be re-defined."

Last February, the second of two Theological Dialogues was held, producing the document, "In Search of Unity." Unfortunately, the Jimmy Creech trial in March diverted attention from the document. However, the 22 participants discovered they had little substantive unity.

United Methodism's *lack* of unity also was painfully illustrated this spring (1998) when 74 members of the Evangelical Renewal Fellowship (ERF) in the California-Nevada Annual Conference asked for a separate organizational entity for evangelicals. Claiming they were "divided beyond reconciliation" from conference leadership, the ERF said separation would allow both sides to pursue their vision for ministry without the "distraction and injury of an ongoing war of ideas." (Two congregations have since left the denomination.)

Following a May 20 meeting in which the evangelical body presented its impassioned request for separation, Bishop Melvin G. Talbert along with his cabinet and staff rejected the request saying separation was unnecessary. They explained, "A strong commitment to inclusion and tolerance welcomes a full range of congregational identities and forms of ministry."

However, when asked about the ERF's complaint that not one evangelical had been appointed to a conference leadership position in years, Bishop Talbert told *World* magazine: "Look, I need to appoint people whom I can trust implicitly, because they represent me." The bishop's statement reflects little "inclusion and tolerance" but rather exclusion and intolerance of evangelicals.

"In search of unity" indeed. But where can it be found? David Mills, director of publishing at Trinity Episcopal School for Ministry, reminds us that neither the unity of the Church nor an effective witness to the world are even possible without a common agreement on doctrine.

Faced with deep divisions on foundational issues, Mills notes that western Anglicanism (and I would add mainline Protestantism in general) seeks unity, unfortunately, in the wrong places.

For example, many look for unity in a *common religious experience*. After all, everyone has some kind of experience with the divine, they say. We just express it differently. The problem, though, is that our religious experiences have become so diverse that it seems we cannot be worshipping the same God. Some find God only in Jesus, while others claim to find him in the female deities of pagan religions or in the depths of their own individual psyches. The problem, says Mills, is that "without a common doctrine, there is no common religious experience, and no unity."

Others seek unity in a *common process*, meaning "dialogue." Unity, say these folks, is not to be found in our answers but in our questions and openness to one another. But dialogue alone, while helpful, cannot bring about unity in the church. Dialogue, if authentic, must eventually come to some conclusion about basic beliefs, about which all parties will either agree or disagree. Without a common doctrine, dialogue will only bring more disagreement.

Another alternative to unifying doctrine is *allegiance to a common institution*. That is, we hope our irreconcilable doctrinal views might somehow be held together by the fact that we all belong to the United Methodist Church. Thus we hear frequent appeals to our "connectional" system and the fact that we are people called United Methodists. However, the unity proves hollow the moment the church has to address a moral or theological issue. Institutional association alone does not unify.

In recent months I have concluded that homosexuality is much more than just a controversial issue facing mainline denominations. It has become a unifying issue for various strains of liberal Protestantism that have no biblical dogma of their own. It is the rallying concern for the liberationists who see persons practicing homosexuality as the new "poor and oppressed," for radical feminists who believe God and biblical morality must be "re-imagined" and the Deity feminized, and for some progressives who believe the Bible is mostly irrelevant amidst today's scientific and technological insights. Serious doctrinal revisionism is often found among those advocating so strongly for the pro-homosexual agenda.

Gordon Wenham is quoted in *Touchstone* cautioning us, however, about what's really at stake in rejecting the biblical witness on homosexuality: "To set aside the biblical teaching on homosexuality...one is not simply eliminating one uncomfortable feature of scriptural teaching. At the same time, the whole biblical teaching on creation, sex, marriage, forgiveness and redemption will be fundamentally altered. The remarks condemning homosexual practice are the tip of an iceberg of biblical theology."

Or, as an openly gay United Methodist pastor once told columnist Terry Mattingly, "This era's fighting is not about six or seven verses on homosexuality. It's about dozens and dozens of verses on marriage and the order of creation. It is time," he said, "for the left to be more honest. It all has to go. It all has to be re-defined." And that is just as we've suspected for a long time.

Unity cannot be found in superficial alternatives such as experience, dialogue, or institutional identity. Only our fidelity to the scriptural revelation and the classic doctrines of the faith can bring about the unity United Methodism so desperately needs.

November/December 1998

Part 3
THE CONTINUING SEXUALITY DEBATE

TWENTY-TWO

Why membership matters

The Scripturalists have historically ranked Scripture above all the other interpretive factors, followed by philosophic reason (nature), scientific reason, and experience. The Experientialists, on the other hand, tend to reconfigure this long-standing hermeneutical ranking by reversing it, giving experience priority.

By the time you read this, our denomination's Judicial Council (our "Supreme Court") will have decided whether to reconsider Decisions 1031 and 1032. These two rulings from last fall overturned punitive disciplinary action against the Rev. Ed Johnson, who had been removed from ministry by the Virginia Annual Conference. The offense: his refusal to receive into membership a man involved in an active homosexual relationship.

The rulings last November brought an immediate (less than 72 hours) response from the United Methodist Council of Bishops in the form of a confusing Pastoral Letter, which, while not stating outright that the bishops disagreed with the Judicial Council's decisions, clearly implied as much. An article in *The New York Times* referred to the Bishops' Pastoral as a "rebuttal" to the Judicial Council. Some bishops voiced vigorous protest.

In recent weeks, the National Association of Schools and Colleges of the United Methodist Church (NASCUMC) made a rare public statement expressing its disagreement about Judicial Council Decision 1032 (the Ed Johnson matter) as well as Decision 1027. The latter upheld the removal of ministerial credentials from Beth Stroud, who had been found guilty in a church trial of being in a lesbian relationship. This group's resolution was approved unanimously in March

by the Division of Higher Education of our General Board of Higher
Education and Ministry.

Judging by the amount of attention these rulings have received,
one senses this is a matter of enormous importance for the church. In
briefs about reconsideration sent on to the Judicial Council, Bishop
Charlene Kammerer (Virginia) states that Article 4 of our Constitution
intends that *no one* be excluded from membership in the UM Church
due to *status*, a term she claims includes homosexual orientation and
practice. In his brief as advocate for the Rev. Ed Johnson, Dr. H. O.
(Tom) Thomas, Jr. disagrees, noting that both Article 4 and Paragraph
214 do speak of "inclusiveness," but this inclusiveness is limited to
those who meet "the requirements" (Par. 138) of the United Methodist
Discipline. All are "eligible" for membership, but not *entitled*.

Bishop Kammerer insists we gladly receive and welcome persons
to our fellowship and congregations who have been baptized members
of other Christian denominations. Thomas says our language here
is contingent—they "may be received." Kammerer believes that the
Discipline does not grant to pastors the "sole discretion" in determin-
ing readiness for membership. Thomas says that nineteenth and twentieth century Methodist *Disciplines* provide "overwhelming evidence"
that historically, pastors have been given discretionary authority to
determine one's readiness for membership.

What is apparent amidst the outcry from various groups and leaders is that this controversy is not just about membership or the discretionary powers of pastors. It is, once again, about homosexual practice.
I don't remember any serious questions about these issues in my 39
years of ministry. Even some liberal pastors have admitted recently
that matters of membership have always been left to the discretion of
the local church pastor. But for many bishops and leaders, they see
neither homosexual orientation *nor practice* as a barrier to membership. However, for many evangelicals, homosexual orientation is not
a barrier, but practice is.

But what is it about the homosexual controversy that makes it so
volatile and divisive? Right now, the unity of five mainline denominations in America is being threatened by it.

Robert Gagnon, author of *The Bible and Homosexual Practice*,
helped me understand better the answer to this question. He says that
in this debate, you have two main camps: the Scripturalists and the
Experientialists. The Scripturalists have historically ranked Scripture

above all the other interpretive factors, followed by philosophic reason (nature), scientific reason, and experience. The Experientialists, on the other hand, tend to reconfigure this long-standing hermeneutical ranking by reversing it, giving experience priority. Gagnon then writes, "Never before in the history of the church has a position so at apparent odds with Scripture gained ascendancy in the church. In any given denomination, should support for committed homosexual practice triumph...it will probably herald for that denomination a decisive paradigm shift in the reorganization of hermeneutical criteria. It will not necessarily knock Scripture off the hermeneutical scale. But it will relegate it to subordinate status, probably placing it at the bottom of the scale" ("Why the disagreement over the biblical witness on homosexual practice?" at RobGagnon.net).

That, it seems to me, is exactly what makes this issue so critical and so potentially divisive. For evangelicals, Scripture cannot, and must never be, relegated to subordinate status on the hermeneutical scale.

May/June 2006

TWENTY-THREE

United Methodism's vows at risk

"Only when persuaded as to the genuineness of their faith and their understanding of and their willingness to observe the rules and regulations of the...Church, shall the Minister receive persons into the fellowship of the church" (Par. 2076).

The Virginia Annual Conference has announced that Bishop Charlene Kammerer and the conference's Board of Ordained Ministry have sent separate petitions to the church's Judicial Council requesting reconsideration of Decisions 1031 and 1032 rendered in the fall of 2005. The Council of Bishops' Pastoral Letter in November 2005 addressed Decision 1032. The letter strongly implied, but did not state explicitly, that the bishops disagreed with the decision. However, the protests of the Judicial Council's decision have been emotional and accusatory ever since. For example:

• Bishop Warner H. Brown Jr. and 124 clergy of the Rocky Mountain Annual Conference signed on to a paid ad that ran in the *Rocky Mountain News* and *The Denver Post*, which said, "We proclaim our vigorous disagreement with this act of injustice by the highest judicial body of our denomination." The decision is an "act of injustice."

• In the California/Nevada Annual Conference, Bishop Beverly Shamana led a protest with a service of Holy Communion and unveiled "An Open Letter to a Brother in Christ Who Was Denied Membership in the Local Church Because of His Sexual Orientation." One wonders if such a letter is being purposefully deceptive in saying he was denied because of his "sexual orientation." Or are the authors simply uninformed? The issue at the heart of this controversy, it must be said again, has to do with homosexual "practice," which our *Discipline* says is "incompatible with Christian teaching," or, simply put, sin.

• Jim Winkler, head of our General Board of Church and Society, went further, detecting sinister motives in those who joined in the Council's majority decision. He charged, "There is an agenda here, and it is to keep gay and lesbian people out of our Church." Never mind that Keith Boyette said in his Concurring Opinion in November that "there is nothing in such language that can remotely be construed...that 'homosexuals' are barred from membership in the church."

In her reasons for requesting reconsideration, Bishop Kammerer states that the 2004 *Book of Discipline* does not "invest discretion in the pastor-in-charge to make the determination of a person's readiness to affirm the vows of membership." She believes the *Discipline* only grants "discretion" in two specific instances, in Paragraphs 216.3 and 224, where the word "discretion" is actually used. The bishop seems chained to literalism here—that is, if the actual word is not used, then pastoral "discretion" cannot be claimed.

What is at stake in this ongoing controversy is the integrity of the church's membership vows. Does anyone who wishes to join, regardless of behavior, practice, or lifestyle, have an unquestioned right to be received into membership? Some say yes, claiming that has always been the church's practice. If so, membership training and vows lose all meaning.

Others of us, however, believe that our *Discipline*'s statement that pastors are ordained to the ministry of Word, Sacrament, Order, and Service is relevant for the debate. Under "Order," pastors are said "to be the administrative officer of the local church" (Par. 340.3.a). In this capacity, they must have—and have had in the past—the authority to determine one's readiness for membership.

Yet some respond as if this idea is brand new for Methodism. Not so. In the 1964 *Discipline* of the Methodist Church, Par. 107 states that "All persons seeking to be saved from their sins...are proper candidates for membership." It goes on to say, "When they shall have given proof of the genuineness of their faith in Christ and of their desire to assume the obligations and become faithful members...[the minister] shall bring them before the congregation, administer the vows," etc.

The 1955 *Discipline* of the Evangelical United Brethren Church has similar language. "The Minister shall instruct all candidates for church membership.... Only when persuaded as to the genuineness of their faith and their understanding of and their willingness to observe the rules and regulations of the...Church, shall the Minister receive persons into the fellowship of the church" (Par. 2076). Our history is clear.

The critical issue emerging in this debate is whether pastors can refuse to receive into membership *any* unrepentant sinner. We are troubled by Bishop Kammerer's claim that neither homosexual "orientation" nor "practice" are barriers to membership. Also, we wonder whether the bishops, through their Pastoral Letter, are insisting that pastors must accept *unrepentant* sinners into the membership of our churches—including those living publicly unchristian lifestyles (i.e., swingers, white supremacists, gay bashers like Fred Phelps, etc.). Surely that is not what they are seeking.

Such a position, were it to prevail, would violate scriptural teaching, our *Book of Discipline*, and the church's great tradition. It would do irreparable harm to the already fragile unity of the United Methodist Church.

March/April 2006

TWENTY-FOUR

The Judicial Council
and the bishops' Pastoral

First, it is regrettable that the Council of Bishops rushed so frantically to respond. One wonders if all the bishops had even read the full text of the decision and had time to process what it said. It seems they hurriedly (within two days of the decision being posted) threw together an unclear and unthoughtful statement.

During the first week of November, just after the Judicial Council posted decisions from its fall meeting, the United Methodist Church hyperventilated.

The Council of Bishops was meeting that week at Lake Junaluska, North Carolina, and went into Executive Session several times to discuss and prepare a "Pastoral Letter," in response particularly to Judicial Council Decision 1032. That decision affirmed that the 2004 *Discipline* "invests discretion in the pastor-in-charge to make the determination of a person's readiness to affirm the vows of membership" (Par. 217). For many United Methodists, this seemed to be a given. Who else other than the senior pastor of a local church is prepared, qualified, and authorized to make such a determination?

In Good News' initial response to the Pastoral Letter, I expressed our disappointment about the lack of clarity in the letter. It has left many United Methodists confused, troubled, and disappointed. While not saying explicitly that they disagreed with Decision 1032, the bishops said things that implied they did, in fact, disagree with it.

The letter seems to agree at one point with the Judicial Council, stating, "While pastors have the responsibility to discern readiness for membership...," but then says just several sentences later, "We also affirm our Wesleyan practice that pastors are accountable to the bishop, superintendent, and the clergy on matters of...membership." Well, which is it? This sends a confusing message.

Again, the Bishops' Pastoral says, "While pastors have the responsibility to discern readiness for membership, homosexuality is not a barrier." This is problematic because it does not clarify whether it means homosexual *orientation* or homosexual *practice*. This is not an insignificant point. The *Discipline* states it is the "practice" which is "incompatible with Christian teaching," not orientation.

But if the Pastoral itself was not clear, individual bishops were crystal clear that they disagreed strongly with the Judicial Council's ruling.

• Bishop Minerva Carcano (Phoenix Area) told her conference in her message accompanying the Pastoral Letter, "That decision was wrong in its interpretation of our beliefs concerning membership in the church." No uncertainty there.

• Bishop John Schol (Washington Area) expressed to his conference, "Methodism is in danger of becoming as pharisaic as the religious leaders during the time of Jesus."

• Bishop Janice Riggle Huie (Texas Conference), who led the writing team for the Council, told *The United Methodist Reporter* that the decision gave the appearance that a pastor can independently exclude homosexuals from membership. "We wanted to make clear that the United Methodist Church is still open to all people," she said.

The lack of clarity in the Pastoral letter is unfortunate, even embarrassing. An article in *The New York Times* described the Pastoral Letter as "a unanimous rebuttal." If the bishops meant for it to be a rebuttal, it is too bad they didn't come out and say so forthrightly. The *Times* article noted that even bishops from socially conservative parts of the country as well as African bishops joined in affirming the statement. (One has trouble believing our African bishops don't see homosexual "practice" as a barrier to membership.)

The truth is, the Pastoral Letter has not been well received across the church. One district superintendent sent it out to his pastors urging them to read it from the pulpit the next Sunday. Several days later, he wrote again cautioning that pastors may want to use their own discretion about whether they read it or not. That could be interpreted as, "the Pastoral Letter has upset a lot of folks so you might want to think twice about reading it publicly."

What, then, might be said about this whole controversy?

First, it is regrettable that the Council of Bishops rushed so frantically to respond. One wonders if all the bishops had even read the full text of the decision and had time to process what it said. It seems they hurriedly threw together an unclear and unthoughtful statement. Their Pastoral Letter was out *within two days* of the decision's posting. One recalls the Council's ten-month silence in 1994 following the heretical and offensive Re-Imagining Conference, as the church waited from January (when the story broke) until November for the Council finally to make an official (and disappointing) response.

Second, it is unfortunate that bishops and other leaders continue to interpret Decision 1032 as one that creates a barrier to all gays and lesbians from being members of the United Methodist Church. One district superintendent wrote to his pastors, "To refuse membership to a person solely on the basis of [his or her] sexual orientation is wrong." Again, orientation is not the issue.

Because of such responses, the Rev. Keith Boyette wrote a Concurring Opinion for the Judicial Council (added to Decision 1032 several days later), "As one can plainly see from the Decision and Digest...as well as the Analysis and Rationale, there is nothing in such language that can remotely be construed as making a sweeping declaration that the Judicial Council has held that 'homosexuals' are barred from membership in the church."

However, Boyette did go on to write that "Par. 138 of the *Discipline* does not support the conclusion that all persons who are willing to give voice to the vows of membership must be received into membership." He cited Par. 138 of the *Discipline*, which states: "In The United Methodist Church inclusiveness means the freedom for the total involvement of all persons who meet the requirements of The United Methodist *Book of Discipline*..." To speak of meeting the "requirements" indicates there are, indeed, substantive requirements to meet in being considered for membership. Without "requirements," membership and vows made publicly before the congregation would mean absolutely nothing.

Third, continued unrepentant homosexual practice creates a problem in one's ability to take the vows of membership with integrity (see vows in Par. 217). One of our bishops has indicated she did not consider either homosexual orientation *or practice* to be a barrier to church membership. That seems, for many United Methodists, to be a problem.

Boyette also addresses this issue in his Concurring Opinion, noting that the local church, through its pastor and agencies, are to hold members accountable (see Par. 221) to the vows of membership outlined in Par. 217. He notes that to receive into membership a person who continued in homosexual practice would result in this conflicted scenario: one would take the vows of membership as per Par. 217, but then immediately be subject to charges as per Par. 221.5 because of one's engaging in a practice that is "incompatible with Christian teaching," which simply means sinful or immoral. The charge cited in Par. 2702.3 is immorality. Such a scenario would be senseless. Any caring pastor would know that such a person is not yet ready for the vows of membership.

John Stott, in his commentary on the book of Romans, cites Bishop Handley Moule, who a century ago said we must "beware equally of an undevotional theology and of an untheological devotion." I fear United Methodism's loss of scriptural authority has left us with "an untheological devotion."

January/February 2006

TWENTY-FIVE

A letter to
Reconciling Ministries Clergy

(The following is a letter of response to an "Open Letter" I received July 21, 2005, from leaders of the Reconciling Ministries Clergy (RMClergy), of the Reconciling Ministries Network (RMN). It included 687 signatures of RMClergy. –JVH)

Dear Revs. Meredith and Aslesen:

Greetings in the Name of Christ the Lord, who calls His Church "to be holy and blameless in his sight."

Your letter of July 15 came as an "Open Letter" to me, copied to United Methodist media. In it you "strongly disagree" with Good News' view that your "Hearts On Fire" conference should not be held at the Lake Junaluska (NC) Assembly over Labor Day 2005. You make your case (to us and the larger church) as to why the conference should go on. Your letter is gracious in tone and opens the door for a thoughtful exchange, which we welcome.

First, some background. In my July/August 2005 editorial in GOOD NEWS magazine, and in my June letter to supporters, I expressed strong concern that the speakers at your conference—including United Methodist Bishops—will join others "to teach, support, encourage, and strategize how to further the *acceptance*" of a practice the church has determined to be "incompatible with Christian teaching." Participants will hear teachings that directly *contradict* Scriptural teaching and the clear, tested standards of our *Book of Discipline*. That should not happen at a United Methodist conference center. Neither should bishops speak. They are responsible for "carrying into effect the rules, regulations, and responsibilities prescribed and enjoined by the General Conference" (Par.47, *Discipline*). They are also charged "with the oversight of the spiritual and temporal affairs of the whole Church" (Par.

427.3). They are not to be dissenters to the church's doctrine or moral teachings.

The stated purpose of the Reconciling Ministries Network cannot be harmonized with either Scripture's or the United Methodist *Book of Discipline*'s teaching about same-sex practice. Yet, the most recent report we have heard is that seven bishops will be participating in this conference. There is no way to measure the negative and demoralizing impact their participation in this event will have on the denomination.

With this background, I will respond briefly to portions of your letter.

First, you reduce the much-debated, critical issue about same-sex practice to being just a matter of "hospitality." But Scriptures come to mind. "But among you there must not be even a hint of sexual immorality, or of any kind of impurity..." (Ephesians 5:3). Again, Paul instructed the Corinthians "not to associate with sexually immoral people" (I Corinthians 5:9). He said he did not mean those "in the world," but meant one "who calls himself a brother but is sexually immoral" (vs. 11). This one should be "put out of your fellowship," Paul said (vs. 2). This and other Scriptures show that "hospitality" is not always the primary virtue.

I did purposefully mention the Reconciling Ministries Network (RMN) website because it states the RMN purpose: "to enable full participation of people of all sexual orientations and gender identities in the life of the United Methodist Church." What is implicit, but not stated outright, is that the RMN views homosexual practice as *normative*, an acceptable alternative for Christians today. "Full participation," then, would include leadership in the church, ordination, and same-sex marriages. This issue is much, much more than just "hospitality."

Second, your letter says, "Advocacy for changing the church's position or teaching. . .has never been understood in United Methodism as grounds for withdrawing hospitality or breaking community." Now let's be clear about what will take place at Lake Junaluska. The "Hearts on Fire" conference will not just be *advocating for change* in the church's standards, it will include large doses of preaching and teaching which are *in direct opposition* to the scriptural norm and to the church's standards. Again, we believe this should not happen.

You say that even Good News exists "to reform, or change, the denomination," implying that the RMN is really just doing what Good News does. But your attempt at equivalency doesn't work.

From the start, Good News has sought to help recover and reaffirm our Wesleyan doctrinal heritage. We have urged fidelity, and thus *continuity*, to our church's long-standing teachings on marriage and Christian morality, which are consistent with the Church's teachings for 2,000 years. On the other hand, the RMN's position advocates *discontinuity* with both Scripture and the Church's long tradition. Following their lead would result in the severance of United Methodism from a major part of its own membership as well as from our larger, ecumenical commitments to the world-wide church (i.e. Catholics, Orthodox, Anglicans, and the Church in the Third-World).

Third, you say that amidst our strong differences, you will "continue to engage in a difficult struggle to discern God's will in this area." This implies that for the RMN, God's will concerning human sexuality is not yet apparent. This is a disturbing claim. It reflects a rejection of Scripture, of two millennia of Church teaching, and 30 years of General Conferences.

We must realize that when human sexuality is severed from its biblical foundation and teaching, then any sexual behavior becomes an option. For without the norm of biblical teaching, there would be no authoritative, corrective word for *any* sexual misbehavior. Any behavior could be justified.

Fourth, your concern about the unity of the United Methodist Church rings hollow. The constant push by many RM Clergy to force local churches to accept a new sexual ethic—affirming homosexual practice—is disturbing and demoralizing to those churches, and has even literally destroyed some.

You cite Wesley's warning about "inward disunion," while at the same time advocating a revisionist view of human sexuality that is itself highly divisive. The new insights and teachings espoused by the RMN have arisen in the church in just the last 30 years or so. You would have the church make a stunning, quite incredible admission: that suddenly, after nearly two millennia of Church history, expansion, and growth, a few of you now have insights and understandings about God's plan for human sexuality that will correct 2,000 years of what must have been erroneous teaching.

It is no surprise that such an audacious claim of new, latter-day understandings has resulted in serious division within the United

Methodist Church. And we would add, such claims in other communions have brought similar division to them as well, including the Presbyterian Church (USA), the Episcopal Church (USA), the Evangelical Lutheran Church of America (ELCA), the United Church of Christ (UCC), and the United Church of Canada, to cite just a few.

Furthermore, you cite the conversation about "schism," or more correctly, "amicable separation," that arose at the 2004 General Conference. What you did not mention is that the catalytic event that brought about the discussion of separation was a late-night conversation between leaders of evangelical caucuses and leaders of the liberal/pro-gay caucuses, including the RMN. We were told by persons representing the RMN view that it really did not matter what General Conference did on the sexuality issues, they would not abide by that action. Such a statement, it must be said, is schismatic. "We will do whatever we want to do, regardless of General Conference" is what we heard being said that night. The question, then, is how can there be a "covenant community" when a group that is supposedly a part of the covenant says it does not intend to abide by the guidelines or terms of the covenant?

Fifth, you mention that many persons across the church "are suffering intensely due to the current policies of the church on homosexuality." Some of us, though, believe that the language of victimization and discrimination represents a misunderstanding of the holy living to which God has called all of us through Christ. If the scriptural teaching about human sexuality is true, reflecting God's revealed will for humankind, then whatever suffering we must endure in amending our lives for righteousness sake will be worth it. And we will be assisted by the grace and power of God. It may not be easy. But he who has called us is faithful and sent the promised Holy Spirit to be our advocate in the midst of the struggle.

Eminent Anglican theologian John Stott's words are particularly relevant here. In his book, *Same-Sex Partnerships? A Christian Perspective,* he writes, "God does indeed accept us just as we are, and we do not have to make ourselves good first; indeed, we cannot. But his 'acceptance' means that he fully and freely forgives all who repent and believe, not that he condones our continuance in sin. Again, it is true that we must accept one another, but only as fellow penitents and fellow pilgrims, not as fellow sinners who are resolved to persist in our sinning...And indeed his offer of friendship to sinners like us is truly wonderful. But he welcomes us in order to redeem and transform us, not to leave us alone in our sins. No acceptance, either by God or by the church, is promised to us if we harden our hearts against God's Word and will. Only judgment."

Finally, in previous issues of GOOD NEWS magazine, we have carried the very timely and poignant words from the renowned German theologian, Wolfhart Pannenberg, and we cite them once again: "Those who urge the church to change the norm of its teaching on this matter must know that they are promoting schism. If a church were to let itself be pushed to the point where it ceased to treat homosexual activity as a departure from the biblical norm. . .such a church would stand no longer on biblical ground but against the unequivocal witness of Scripture. A church that took this step would cease to be the one, holy, catholic, and apostolic church" (from *Church Times* in Britain).

In light of Pannenburg's prophetic warning, it is surprising how many RM Clergy still march steadily on, determined to reconstruct the Church's long-held teaching on human sexuality—with seemingly little or no awareness that they are traveling a schismatic path that could destroy the unity and apostolicity of our church. That is not what we elders promised to do when we were ordained.

For these and other reasons, we do not believe the "Hearts on Fire" conference can be a time of "healing the brokenness," either in the lives of individuals, or in the larger church. Authentic healing comes as the Holy Spirit works in us through the faithful preaching and teaching of the Word of God. Healing comes when we allow the light of God's Word and truth to shine upon the dark crevices of our lives, letting his transforming grace make us new creatures in Christ. Faithful discipleship means adhering to and obeying Scripture and God's plan for our lives. It does not allow an altering of that plan according to human whim, personal preference, or cultural trend.

We remain convinced that the planned theme and emphases of the "Hearts on Fire" conference, as publicized on the RMN website ,contradict the clear teachings of Scripture and the carefully developed standards of the United Methodist *Book of Discipline*. For that reason, the event should not be held at a church-owned and supported conference center such as Lake Junaluska.

Once again, I am appreciative of the tone of your letter and for the occasion it has provided to exchange views about this important matter. I hope this might lead to further, cordial but candid exchanges in the future.

In Christ's Name,
James V. Heidinger II / President and Publisher

September/October 2005

TWENTY-SIX

Learning from the Stroud trial

*One wonders just how many times this claim
has been repeated by well-meaning people across
America, even in the church. It is the supposed
"consensus of the scientific community," we are
told. The only problem with this claim is that it is
not supported with scientific evidence.*

United Methodists are indebted to the trial court that met near
Philadelphia in early December 2004 to hear the case against
the Rev. Beth Stroud. By vote of 12-1, the jury found Stroud guilty
of engaging in practices which the church has declared incompatible
with Christian teaching. By a closer vote (7-6), jurors acted to remove
her ministerial credentials.

Beth Stroud is obviously a gifted person who has related well with
those to whom she has ministered. However, personal effectiveness
was not the issue in her trial, but rather, fidelity to the established
standards of the United Methodist Church.

Our guidelines on sexuality have been worked out prayerfully and
carefully over the past 20 years. They are faithful to Scripture, consistent with the church's historic teaching, and compassionate toward
all. To establish its standards, the church has utilized Christian conferencing as well as can be done, given the size of General Conference
legislative committees and plenary sessions.

In this unpleasant matter, the church was well served by Bishop
Peter Weaver, who was, until this summer, bishop for Eastern
Pennsylvania and for Beth Stroud. As a witness for the church's counsel, Weaver testified he had learned of Stroud's lesbian relationship
in a meeting with her in 2003. After seeking various pastoral options
that would avoid a trial, which Stroud rejected, Weaver filed a com-

plaint against her.

Retired Bishop Joseph Yeakel presided over a fair trial. He is to be commended for refusing to allow Stroud's defense team to present six expert witnesses who were set to challenge the church's policy on homosexuality. His ruling was correct. The church's standards were not on trial—Beth Stroud's lesbian relationship was. Many United Methodists were disappointed, however, that Bishop Yeakel commented to an observer following the trial that the church would one day have to apologize to Beth Stroud for what it had done. This unfortunate, inappropriate comment from the presiding judge got passed on to the media in a post-trial press conference.

Stroud's defense counsel, Dr. Dennis Williams, stated early that he hoped the trial would be a "learning moment for all of us." Perhaps it will be.

Though the defense team could not present their case against the church's standards during the trial, they did release their arguments to the media when the court was in recess. One of their arguments claimed that "it is the consensus of the scientific community that homosexuality is a status." It claimed that homosexual conduct is inseparable from this status or orientation and cannot be excluded because it is based on "an unchangeable personal characteristic."

Whoa, wait a moment here. One wonders just how many times this claim has been repeated by well-meaning people across America, even in the church. It is the supposed "consensus of the scientific community," we are told. The only problem with this claim is that it is not supported with scientific evidence.

Yes, let's make this a "learning moment." The Opinion Research Corporation recently asked 1,072 practicing psychiatrists for their views on various aspects of sexuality; 207 responded. When asked if homosexuals could be changed to heterosexuals, 53 percent responded "yes," 24 percent were "not sure," and only 22 percent said "no."

Dr. Ruth Tiffany Barnhouse, who was professor of psychiatry and pastoral care at the Perkins School of Theology, does not buy this supposed scientific consensus. In *Homosexuality: A Symbolic Confusion* (Seabury), she wrote, "Approximately thirty percent of male homosexuals who come to psychotherapy for *any reason* can be converted to the heterosexual adaptation."

In an article for the *Circuit Rider*, Dr. Barnhouse argues, "The frequent claim by 'gay' activists that it is impossible for homosexuals to change their orientation is categorically untrue. Such a claim accuses scores of conscientious, responsible psychiatrists and psychologists of falsifying their data."

The supposed "consensus of the scientific community"—that homosexuality is inborn and unchangeable—is purely a mythical claim kept alive by endless, non-critical repetition.

The final word in this "learning moment," of course, must be God's. Nowhere in Scripture is there *any* textual support for homosexual coupling. In his book *Same Sex Partnerships?*, Dr. John Stott sums it up well: "...the love quality of gay relationships is not sufficient to justify them. Indeed...they are incompatible with true love because they are incompatible with God's law. Love is concerned for the highest welfare of the beloved. And our highest human welfare is found in obedience to God's law and purpose, not in revolt against them."

We need more "learning moments" from God's unchanging Word.

January/February 2005

TWENTY-SEVEN

Thinking clearly about homosexuality

Byrd also cited established researchers — such as Byne and Parsons and Friedman and Downey — who have reviewed the studies linking biology and homosexual attraction. They concluded that there was no evidence to support an innate, biological theory.

Recent church dialogues about homosexuality have convinced me we are missing the real issue we should be discussing.

In these dialogues, I've heard articulate and sincere persons tell how they came to their personal understanding that they were "gay" or "lesbian." With conviction, they tell how they became convinced "This is who I really am. This is how God made me. I cannot change."

These stories are affirmed by some pastors and laypersons, who are eager to give compassionate support. They, too, express certainty that gays and lesbians are born this way and cannot change. This view gained momentum more than 20 years ago when one of our bishops wrote his pastors, telling them he believed homosexuality was "a mysterious gift of God's grace."

Now the matter that never gets discussed in our church dialogues is the *presuppositional* question: Is homosexuality, in fact, innate (inborn, genetic, biologically caused) and immutable (unchangeable), or is it not?

In the March/April 2003 issue of GOOD NEWS, A. Dean Byrd and two associates examine the innate-immutability argument about homosexual attraction. Byrd is vice president of the National Association for Research and Therapy of Homosexuality (NARTH) and is a trained scientist and licensed clinical psychologist. In this article, Byrd states that "Scientific attempts to demonstrate that homosexual attraction is biologically (innately) determined have failed." Much of Byrd's evidence comes from scientists who are themselves homosexual and lesbian.

For example, Dean Hamer, a gay researcher, tried to link male homosexuality to a stretch of DNA located at the tip of the X chromosome, but failed. He concluded, "Homosexuality is not purely genetic...environmental factors play a role. There is not a single master gene that makes people gay."

Byrd cites Simon LeVay, a homosexual scientist whose studies comparing the brains of homosexual and heterosexual men received dramatic coverage in *Time* magazine years ago. Commenting on his work, LeVay admitted, "It's important to stress what I didn't find. I did not prove that homosexuality is genetic, or find a genetic cause for being gay. I didn't show that gay men are born that way, the most common mistake people make in interpreting my work."

Byrd also cited established researchers such as Byne and Parsons and Friedman and Downey who have reviewed the studies linking biology and homosexual attraction. They concluded that there was no evidence to support an innate, biological theory. They claimed, rather, that homosexuality is best explained by a model where "temperamental and personality traits interact with the familial and social milieu as the individual's sexuality emerges."

Byrd also notes lesbian activist biologist Dr. Anne Fausto-Sterling of Brown University, who says about the biological argument: "It's bad science and bad politics. It seems to me that the way we consider homosexuality in our culture is an ethical and a moral question." And we would add, it's a theological question as well.

Byrd's conclusion is that the innate-immutability claim "finds no basis in science." Yet many United Methodist pastors continue telling their parishioners, with apparent authority and competence, that we must accept the practice of homosexuality on those grounds. One of our bishops even claimed in his conference paper that being homosexual is "no different than being left-handed."

In the church's debate on this issue, we need to claim our Lord's promise when he said, "And you shall know the truth, and the truth shall make you free" (John 8:32). At the 2000 General Conference, Good News distributed a sampling of comments from 14 of some 36 mental health authorities who have spent years treating persons struggling with problems of sexuality, including homosexuality.

These eminent professionals, psychiatrists and psychologists, are respected practitioners who report from years of experience. They include persons such as Reuben Fine, Edmund Bergler, Irving Bieber, Lawrence Hatterer, Arthur Janov, Charles Socarides, Masters and Johnson, Robert Kronemeyer, Mansell Pattison, Gerard van den Aardweg, Ruth Tiffany Barnhouse, William P. Wilson, and others. The truth is, success rates of persons reverting from homosexuality to heterosexuality varied from 28 percent to a high of 71.6 percent. These professionals attest that there is nothing immutable about homosexuality. Persons have and are changing.

Ruth Tiffany Barnhouse sums it up well, insisting, "The frequent claim by 'gay' activists that it is impossible for homosexuals to change their orientation is categorically untrue." The sad reality is that such claims only diminish the desire of persons to seek help in leaving homosexual behavior. Scientific data simply does not support the innate-immutable claim.

March/April 2003

TWENTY-EIGHT

The need for fidelity in leadership

When United Methodist bishops and pastors advocate the acceptance of homosexual practice as normative and affirm same-sex covenants, they are not being faithful to their vows of ordination and consecration.

On June 15, 2001, the Rev. Mark Williams, pastor of Woodland Park UM Church in Seattle acknowledged to his colleagues in the Pacific Northwest Annual Conference that he was a "practicing gay man." Nearly 12 months later, on May 30 of this year, a committee on investigation of that conference dismissed a complaint against Williams. He will not face a church trial and will continue as pastor of the Woodland congregation.

The United Methodist Church seems to have the remarkable capacity to find new ways of shooting itself in the foot. Here a conference committee on investigation received a complaint initiated by the bishop against a pastor who had acknowledged before *the entire annual conference* that he was a "practicing gay man"! When the committee finally met eleven months later, it asked Williams the obligatory question mandated by Judicial Council Decision 920 about whether he "is engaged in genital sexual acts with a person of the same gender." (This was included to guarantee fairness, in the case of any misunderstanding.) Williams simply refused to answer the question. With that, the investigating body announced it "found there was not reasonable cause to forward this matter for a church trial." The ruling surprised even Williams' supporters and sympathizers.

What we have here is a particular situation that illustrates perfectly the message sent by delegates at the Western Jurisdictional Conference in July of 2000. In a defiant statement, "We Will Not Be Silent," approved almost unanimously by delegates there, the Western

Jurisdiction was saying officially that it disagreed with the votes at General Conference 2000 affirming the *Discipline's* standards on homosexuality.

"We cannot accept discrimination against gay, lesbian, bisexual or transgender persons and, therefore, we will work toward their full participation at all levels in the life of the church and society (meaning homosexual ordination and same-sex covenants)," the Western Jurisdiction statement said. This, of course, is nothing new for the Western Jurisdiction.

For a committee on investigation to allow Williams not to answer the question about whether he was involved in same-gender sexual activity is simply an abdication of duty. In a criminal case, persons may "take the fifth" to avoid self-incrimination. But they don't have that option in civil cases, and neither should they in a church hearing, where we are committed to maintaining the "highest standards of holy living" (*Discipline*, Par. 304.3).

This entire sordid matter comes at a time when the Roman Catholic Church is under enormous public criticism for failing to uphold and enforce its teachings on sexual ethics. Richard John Neuhaus, editor of *First Things* journal, writing in the June/July 2002 issue, has words that are hauntingly relevant for United Methodists. He says the crisis in the Catholic Church is about three things: fidelity, fidelity, and fidelity.

First, writes Neuhaus, "The fidelity of bishops and priests to the teaching of the Church and to their solemn vows." Let's remember that Rev. Williams took public vows upon entering the ministry, we assume voluntarily and carefully, in which he said he had studied the church's teachings, agreed with them, and would be faithful in teaching them. Sadly, he must not have meant what he promised.

Second, "The fidelity of bishops in exercising oversight in ensuring obedience to that teaching and to those vows," Neuhaus says. And let's remember, it is a stated Presidential Duty (*Discipline*, Par. 415.2) of United Methodist bishops "to ensure that the annual conference and general church policies and procedures are followed." Bishop Galvan should have instructed both Williams and the committee on investigation that the question about same-gender sexual activity must be answered. What happened was a charade that made a mockery of our system.

Third, says Neuhaus, "Fidelity of the lay faithful in holding bishops and priests accountable." Many United Methodists are beginning to wonder if we have the institutional mechanisms for holding bishops (and pastors for that matter) accountable. We must keep trying.

Why do some priests not live by their solemn oaths of chastity and celibacy, Neuhaus asks. His answer sounds all too familiar: "Because bishops turned a blind eye to what seminarians were being taught; or, even worse, bishops by their own example indicated that sacred vows do not really mean what they really say, and what the Church says they mean." He went on to say the Church's academic and theological dissent on sexuality has served only to "issue permission slips for an era of wink-wink, nudge-nudge, the consequences of which are now on scandalous public display."

When United Methodist bishops and pastors advocate the acceptance of homosexual practice as normative and affirm same-sex covenants, they are not being faithful to their vows of ordination and consecration. They are undermining the integrity of the church by encouraging behavior explicitly forbidden by their church's official teaching.

July/August 2002

TWENTY-NINE

Science has not trumped God's wisdom

In an article in Perspectives in Human Sexuality, *Dr. John W. Money, PhD., widely recognized professor at Johns Hopkins School of Medicine, said, "Whatever may be the possible unlearned assistance from constitutional sources, the child's psychosexual identity is not written, unlearned, in the genetic code, the hormonal system or the nervous system at birth."'*

General Conference has come and gone. Delegates spoke persua-sively with 65 to 74 percent affirming our church's historic stan-dards on the votes concerning homosexuality. Still, the challenges to the church's position continue.

Just prior to General Conference, Bishops Joe Sprague and Sharon Rader tried unsuccessfully to get a resolution through the Council of Bishops. They wanted the Council to ask the 2000 General Conference to find "faithful pastoral and administrative ways to affirm gay and lesbian United Methodists and neither condemn homosexual orien-tation *per se* nor reject candidates for representative ministry solely on the basis of sexual orientation..." (It should be noted that it is not "orientation" that is addressed in the *Discipline*, but "practice.")

Part of the reason for their attempted resolution, said Sprague and Rader, was "our understandings of continually emerging biological and psychological data that sexual orientation is not a chosen life-style but an inherent reality..." When you hear such a reference in any future conversation, let me urge you to please call time-out and politely ask to see that data and its documentation. Why? Because there is virtually no supportive data for such claims. Yet, we regularly hear: "This is how God made me" or "I was born gay. It is who I am." As Richard John Neuhaus would say, that view has everything going for it except empirical evidence. (A study by gay researcher Simon LeVey got major coverage in *Time* magazine a few years ago, but it was soon discounted by the scientific community.)

I realize that empirical evidence alone is not adequate in such a critical moral debate. For evangelicals, the biblical account provides for us God's clear intent when he created humankind. But it does help Christians to know, as the debate continues, that recent "emerging biological and psychological data" have *not* come along to trump the wisdom of God.

We need to hear some of the respected voices who have spoken about this:

• Dr. William Byrne, resident of psychiatry at Columbia University's College of Physicians and Surgeons, says: "The public is now getting the impression that there's this mountain of evidence being built to support the idea that homosexuality is biological. But in fact what we're seeing is a stream of zeros being added together."

• Dr. John W. Money, PhD., widely recognized professor at Johns Hopkins School of Medicine, said in an article in *Perspectives in Human Sexuality*: "Whatever may be the possible unlearned assistance from constitutional sources, the child's psychosexual identity is not written, unlearned, in the genetic code, the hormonal system, or the nervous system at birth."

• Eminent psychiatrist, Dr. Charles Socarides, of the Albert Einstein College of Medicine in New York, says, "Homosexuality, the choice of a partner of the same sex for orgiastic satisfaction, is not innate..." And again, "The major challenge in treating homosexuality...has, of course, been the misconception that the disorder is innate or inborn."

• Masters and Johnson, the most widely known authorities in the field of human sexual behavior, have written: "The genetic theory of homosexuality has been generally discarded today."

• David F. Greenberg's massive study, *The Construction of Homosexuality*, looked at every significant culture from the beginning of recorded history, examining how homosexuality was expressed. He challenges the idea that homosexuality should be seen as a "biological given," and urges, instead, that we stress much more that homosexuality is a behavior.

Greenberg's conclusion is also the view of Dr. Paul Cameron who heads the Family Research Institute in Colorado Springs. (Be sure to see his web site at www.familyresearchinst.org.) He favors the historic definition of homosexuality—that just as "a smoker" is a person who smokes, so "a homosexual" is a person who engages in homosexual activity. He believes this definition is consistent with the bulk of scientific evidence and makes a persuasive case in his June/July (2000) *Report*. Cameron suggests that the "genetic" or "constitutional" argument is a way of controlling the linguistic terms of the debate. It is part of "the attempt by homosexual activists to create a new social reality, a class of 'victims of irresistible benign sexual urges.'" And then, to disagree with their behavior is tantamount to denying their personhood.

Ex-gay ministry leader Alan Medinger says in an article, "You Are Not A Homosexual," that homosexual identity is an "artificial category" and adds, "we have long urged people not to define themselves by their particular sins or forms of brokenness."

The truth is, the claim that homosexuality is innate or inborn, while foundational to the gay rights movement, has virtually no empirical support.

September/October 2000

THIRTY

Reflections on the
Bishops' Pastoral Letter

The bishops make clear that they "hear the anguish of many gay and lesbian persons, their parents and families." We hope they also hear the pain and anguish of faithful United Methodists who feel alienated from their church and its leaders and are disillusioned that their leaders can't give clear leadership on this controversial matter.

The United Methodist Council of Bishops' Pastoral Letter released November 5 (1999) contains much the church should affirm. We urge local churches to read it carefully, to study and discuss it in Sunday school classes and small groups, and to give feedback to their bishops when appropriate. In the Letter's spirit of conferencing, we offer these reflections in response.

First we would applaud the opening statement of the Letter in which the bishops bring greetings "in the name of Jesus Christ who alone is our salvation, our hope, and our peace." We commend this important claim concerning the uniqueness of Jesus Christ as the *only* savior and hope for the world.

Second we appreciate the bishops' word that it is time to focus attention on the church's primary mission of making disciples of Jesus Christ. The church has, indeed, been distracted, demoralized, and diminished by the continued public debate on homosexuality. Unfortunately, the church has been distracted by public statements of bishops who cannot affirm the present standards in The Book of Discipline, as well as by the efforts of United Methodist boards and agencies to change the denomination's standards. These distractions have exacted a heavy toll on church membership and morale.

Third we are pleased the bishops have joined with many others who are calling for concerted prayer, fasting, and conversation as we prepare for General Conference in Cleveland. Our divided church needs this kind of earnest fasting and prayer.

Fourth we applaud the bishops' plans to initiate periods of "Christian conferencing" with their respective delegations to General Conference and at future meetings of the Council. We hope, however, that conferencing will not be seen as a new authority for United Methodism that seeks new and different answers than what we have understood and affirmed from Scripture about God's plan for male and female, for marriage and sexuality.

Fifth we share the bishops' concern that the controversy about homosexuality could lead to division within the church. We applaud the bishops in their desire "to lead the church faithfully, and to be a witness to the unity of the Spirit." We are saddened, however, that the trumpet of episcopal leadership gives an uncertain sound on this issue. The present standards in *The Book of Discipline* concerning homosexuality have been forged carefully over the last seven quadrennia, the result of reasoned, prayerful study and Christian conferencing. Unfortunately, the Bishops' Letter does not affirm those standards with any sense of conviction, nor does it acknowledge them as consistent with the standards of most all other communions of Christ's Church. Instead, it approaches the matter as if it were still unsettled and waiting for resolution. The bishops seem unwilling to accept the verdict of the church, which has decided clearly and convincingly on the issue but perhaps not in the way some bishops had wished.

Sixth we acknowledge the value of a call to "be quiet, to be united, to listen for God's guiding voice, and to learn from one another." We are concerned, however, that this could be misunderstood. When the church is facing a crisis over a major moral issue, it is not a time only to be quiet. It is also a time to speak lovingly, truthfully, and scripturally on behalf of the church's moral teaching. Unity should characterize the body of Christ, but the church must never seek its unity at the expense of truth.

Seventh we join the bishops in condemning hate language and mean-spiritedness in the on-going debate about homosexuality. Angry, hateful language and name-calling (whether "queers and fags" or "homophobes and heterosexists") have no part in the church's conversations. The bishops make clear that they "hear the anguish of many gay and lesbian persons, their parents and families." We hope they also hear the pain and anguish of faithful United Methodists who feel alienated from their church and its leaders and are disillusioned by their leaders' inability to give clear leadership on this controversial matter.

Eighth the Pastoral Letter is sensitive to the "anguish of many gay and lesbian persons" and speaks of fulfilling "the biblical mandate of hospitality" for all persons. However, the letter fails to affirm the integrity of those who thoughtfully and prayerfully embrace the denomination's present standards. Many believe those standards do, indeed, reflect a church attempting "to respond in Christian love."

Finally we affirm the bishops' desire to keep the church focused on making disciples. We are concerned, however, with the implication that the church's struggle over homosexuality is unrelated to disciple-making. The church must face the critical question of whether one desiring to be a faithful disciple can at the same time actively engage in homosexual practice. It seems clear to us that Scripture and the church's long tradition say "no."

January/February 2000

Part 4
FAITHFULNESS IN OVERSIGHT

THIRTY-ONE

UMW/Renew Conversation: A good start

I was proud of our Renew team—Faye Short, Carolyn Elias, Janice Crouse, Katy Kiser, Liza Kittle, and Ruth Velasquez. They had prayed much, prepared carefully, and articulated graciously, with poise yet firmness, the concerns we have had for many years about programs and policies of the Women's Division.

"This discussion of controversial issues between those of us who are biblically orthodox and the women of the denomination's leadership will be a historic debate—the first time our two different perspectives have been aired publicly face-to-face," said Faye Short, President of the Renew Network, the women's program arm of Good News.

And so it was. On Wednesday, September 21, several hundred persons gathered in the Chapel of Wesley Theological Seminary, in Washington, D.C., to be a part of a structured conversation between the two groups.

In opening statements, Jan Love, Deputy General Secretary of the Women's Division, said she hoped the day would serve as a "model" for the church, with people coming together and listening to one another. Faye Short thanked the Women's Division for accepting the invitation to debate publicly and expressed hope the meeting would bring about "widespread conversation" in the church.

We hope much follow-up conversation takes place, and I believe it will. In fact, the entire event was web cast and could be viewed on the United Methodist Women's website, along with a complete transcript of the exchange. Articles may also be seen on RENEW's website. A DVD/video will soon be available from RENEW, along with a packet of supplemental materials, to assist women in our local churches to pursue further the issues dealt with in the conversation, plus other issues that went unaddressed.

I was proud of our RENEW team—Faye Short, Carolyn Elias, Janice Crouse, Katy Kiser, Liza Kittle, and Ruth Velasquez. They had prayed much, prepared carefully, and articulated graciously, with poise and resolve, the concerns we have had for many years about programs and policies of the Women's Division.

One cannot fully understand the context of this conversation without understanding it is the result of the RENEW Network's "Call For Reform" of the Women's Division, an initiative launched in 2001, also endorsed by the Good News board of directors. In December of 2001, Faye Short published a 28-page White Paper titled "Our Basis For Concern," which documents six long-standing issues that have been concerns of the RENEW Network and Good News.

The issues cited and documented thoroughly in "Our Basis For Concern" include the Women's Division's 1) pro-abortion position; 2) endorsement of homosexual/lesbian practice; 3) involvement and continued support of the 1993 Re-Imagining Conference; 4) questionable theological teaching and social justice mission concept; 5) support of a politically left-leaning ideology; and 6) autonomy/accountability issues.

The White Paper acknowledges that "United Methodist Women and its predecessor groups have done immeasurable good through works of Christian love and service around the world—and still do." There is no denying that. But it goes on to document the above six issues that indicate how out of touch the Women's Division's views are with the majority of United Methodist women at the local church level. Our women—and pastors too—need to be engaged on these issues in the "widespread conversation" that Faye Short hoped would result.

For the sake of specificity, let me cite a few concerns.

• The Women's Division's long-standing pro-abortion position. At the 1992 spring meeting of the Women's Division, postcards were provided at each table for attendees to pick up and mail to their senators in support of the Freedom of Choice Act, which, in the form endorsed at this meeting, went far beyond *Roe v. Wade* in support of no restrictions whatsoever on abortion.

In 1996, the Women's Division endorsed a letter sent by the

Religious Coalition for Reproductive Choice (RCRC) expressing agreement with President Clinton's action that vetoed the strongly-supported, bi-partisan bill that would have banned the gruesome procedure of partial-birth abortion, and even urged Congress not to override the veto.

Coming well after the White Paper was published was the April 25, 2004 "March for Women's Lives" in Washington, D.C. The Women's Division gave this massive pro-abortion rally its unqualified endorsement and even contributed $5,000 to help underwrite expenses for the march. Major organizers of the event included Planned Parenthood, the National Organization for Women (NOW), the Feminist Majority, and the American Civil Liberties Union (ACLU).

• The Women's Division's support for homosexual practice. At the 1988 General Conference, a minority report was submitted which attempted to remove the "incompatible with Christian teaching" phrase from the *Discipline*, and replace it with "We find mixed testimony about the practice of homosexuality in Scripture, tradition, and in the human sciences." The first signature on the minority report was that of Sally Ernst, then national president of United Methodist Women.

Again, an article in the July/August issue of *Response* magazine by J. Ann Craig, Executive Secretary for Spiritual and Theological Development, identified Christian Fundamentalists [there's that term again] as those who "...use terms and beliefs to promote the subservience of women, deny reproductive freedom [abortion], label homosexuality as sin...." What this means is that pro-life Christians and United Methodists who agree with the church's position on homosexual practice are "fundamentalists" in the most negative sense of the term. (Jan Love did say in the conversation that RENEW, Good News, and the Institute on Religion and Democracy are not religious extremists, nor are they fundamentalists, according to the definition she used. However, the statement by J. Ann Craig noted above *would* include those of us in the above three renewal groups.) In today's discourse, calling someone "fundamentalist" is a descriptive, ecclesial put-down. It is a demeaning and dismissive term.

• The Women's Division's support for the 1993 Re-Imagining Conference. The White Paper reminds us that this radical conference, attended by numerous UMW staff, directors, and some conference officers at Division expense, focused its worship on Sophia;

stood in solidarity with Christian lesbians; and denied the necessity of Christ's atoning death. It goes on to say that "at no time has the Division denounced the deviant theology of Re-Imagining or discouraged participation in the Re-Imagining Community (which is now defunct)." In fact, Division officer, J. Ann Craig, was one of nine women who drafted the document "A Time of Hope—A Time of Threat," in defense of Re-Imagining.

• The Women's Division's questionable theological teaching and social justice mission concepts. In the February 1991 issue of *Response* magazine, an article entitled "Was Jesus Born to Die?" answered its own title with a "no." The death of Jesus was not seen by author John Baron as pre-planned by God and necessary for the provision of salvation of humankind.

Again, the November 2000 issue of *Response* was devoted to "Interfaith Challenge—Interfaith Response." The issue conveyed the concept that all religions are equally redemptive, and, as one article put it, "Christian faith must see itself as *one* of the religious options for the Peoples of the world."

These are just a few of many quite specific concerns in Faye Short's "Our Basis For Concern," a document that covers concerns spanning more than two decades. This well-documented White Paper would be just the right place for that future "widespread conversation" to begin.

November / December 2005

THIRTY-TWO

Are we serious about missions?

Earlier in the last century, United Methodism fielded some 2,500 standard support, full-time missionaries. In 1965, we had more than 1,500 career overseas missionaries. When we ran the "Missions Derailed" article in 1983, GBGM's numbers had dropped to only 453 career overseas missionaries (GBGM staff, both executive and support, at the time totaled 458).

Twenty years ago, GOOD NEWS ran a major cover story titled "Missions Derailed" (May/June, 1983). After a six-month investigative study, we voiced concern that the General Board of Global Ministries (GBGM), United Methodism's official mission agency, was failing in its church-mandated assignment.

Our report cited problems such as excessive administrative overhead, a decline in the number of standard support overseas missionaries, and a change in the theological underpinnings of the board's work. We were concerned that the board had moved from a traditional understanding of mission to the trendy new liberation theology—a strange mixture of radical politics and liberal religion that views salvation as "liberating" persons from unjust social structures.

What brought this whole matter to mind was a recent United Methodist News Service (11/3/03) piece noting that "budget woes" will mean no new full-time missionaries appointed in 2004. But what jumped out in the story was the report that after non-renewal of contracts, retirements, and requests not to be reassigned, GBGM *is left with just some 287 "in the category of standard support missionaries."* Only 287!

Let me provide some context. Earlier in the last century, United Methodism fielded some 2,500 standard support, full-time missionaries. In 1965, we had more than 1,500 career overseas missionaries. When we ran the "Missions Derailed" article in 1983, GBGM's numbers had dropped to only 453 career overseas missionaries (GBGM staff, both executive and support, at the time totaled 458).

One of our concerns as early as 1972, when the Evangelical Missions Council was formed and later became an arm of Good News for eight years (until 1984), was that United Methodism appeared to be going out of the mission-sending business. We were always told that wasn't the case. Today, however, GBGM has just 287 standard support missionaries, with no plans to take on any new ones in 2004.

Further context may be even more helpful. In 1983, when we had 453 missionaries, the Southern Baptist Foreign Mission Board had some 3,196 career overseas missionaries, served by around 300 headquarters staff.

These trends at GBGM, plus a loss of a vital theology of mission, added to the board's rejection of many evangelical applicants who were left with no choice but to seek service under other mission-sending agencies, led to the formation twenty years ago of The Mission Society, headquartered in Norcross, Georgia. The new, unofficial sending agency has always seen itself as a "supplemental" sending body, and has always urged that its support be from the members' second-mile mission giving, not from their churches' apportionments.

Despite being viewed condescendingly by many denominational leaders as the black sheep of United Methodism's institutional family, The Mission Society, after just twenty years, *now has 156 missionaries (full-time, career) serving in 29 countries on five continents*, with a budget of just $9 million and a staff of only 25. Its ministries are holistic, culturally sensitive, and involve more than 3,000 national citizens in countries of missionary involvement.

I have also been following with appreciation the efforts of the United Methodist Missionary Association, chaired now by Norma Kehrberg. This unofficial group of more than 350 current and retired UM missionaries seeks input into GBGM's mission policies and strategies. They have expressed concern about the board's diminishing missionary force. In 2001, they even called on directors to initiate a "major review" of GBGM.

Our mission board has a mandate: "To challenge all United

Methodists with the New Testament imperative to proclaim the gospel to the ends of the earth...and to recruit, send, and receive missionaries" (*Discipline*, Par. 1302.1, 3).

Twenty years ago, a GBGM official said the World Division had as its "controlling principle" in the 1980s the "empowerment of the poor and the oppressed." Former GBGM head, Randy Nugent, also called back then for a new form of missionary outreach that should be a "mission to those who are at the levers of economic and social affairs."

While caring for the poor is an essential element to the gospel message, we cannot fail to simultaneously offer the saving message of Jesus Christ. Social justice and preaching the gospel should never be pitted against one another. Yet the board did that very thing. It failed tragically in its missionary mandate.

Does the United Methodist mission agency, under its new leadership, have the will and passion to fulfill its biblical and disciplinary mandate? Do its leaders affirm the New Testament imperative of the Great Commission, or do they believe simply that all will be saved? Is Christ the Savior for all the world, or are all the world's religions equally valid and efficacious?

Their answers to these important questions will determine whether those tragic, decreasing numbers change.

January/February 2004

THIRTY THREE

The role of gatekeepers

"Bishops are the appointed custodians of the doctrine, discipline, and teaching of the church. They are to hold the church—its pastors, staff, and laity—accountable for the faith, order, doctrine and discipline of the church. And this task must include their colleagues on the Council of Bishops."

Last year (2001) was a bad year, writes James M. Kushiner, executive editor of *Touchstone* journal, in a recent editorial.

His litany of bad things included the September 11 terrorist attacks, which found America's intelligence and security organizations unprepared to protect us, even when given information about possible terrorist plans.

He adds to that the Enron scandal, with dishonest executives profiting while workers lost jobs and retirement funds. Some CPAs for Arthur Andersen, hired to guard and oversee the integrity of the company's financial reports, hid the truth and deceived investors.

Finally, he notes the clergy sexual abuse scandals that hit the Catholic Church, with more than 250 priests having to resign or be removed. About the latter, Kushiner says, "Those entrusted with the protection of the flock let the predators harm their charges... Just like the CIA and FBI and Arthur Andersen, the bishops, the security guards of the church, were at best, asleep, at worse, criminally complicit." Gatekeepers didn't do their jobs.

The United Methodist Church needs courageous and faithful gatekeepers. We have generally understood that to be the task of our pastors and bishops. When pastors are ordained, they are asked if they will both preach the Word of God faithfully and defend the church against all doctrine contrary to God's Word. The assumption is that such "contrary" doctrine exists and the faithful should not be subjected to it.

For United Methodist bishops, the consecration liturgy asks, "Will you guard the faith, order, liturgy, doctrine, and discipline of the Church against all that is contrary to God's word?" So they, too, solemnly promise to guard the Church "against all that is contrary to God's word." Our pastors and bishops serve as gatekeepers.

This gatekeeping responsibility is profoundly important, especially for bishops. Being elected and consecrated a bishop is not just an honor bestowed on an effective or popular pastor. Nor is it just the next step up in one's professional career. It is, or should be, a divine "setting apart" to the critical task of being an overseer and gatekeeper of the church. Bishops are the appointed custodians of the doctrine, discipline, and teaching of the church. They are to hold the church—its pastors, staff, and laity—accountable for the faith, order, doctrine, and discipline of the church. And this task must include their colleagues on the Council of Bishops.

Kushiner rightly notes that the task of a gatekeeper is difficult, demanding, and even dangerous. No one would hire police who are afraid to use their guns, intelligence agents worried about popularity, airport security guards who won't turn people away, or public accountants who think bookkeeping is just a matter of being clever in cooking the books. No, the standards are higher for all who are gatekeepers. We expect unwavering honesty and relentless integrity from them.

But above all, the church needs fidelity and integrity in its gatekeepers. In every age, the church is threatened by those outside who would harm and destroy, and by those within who would accommodate the church to secular norms or harm the faithful by teaching false doctrine. Pastors can become predators and deceive their flock, causing great harm.

So, both our United Methodist clergy as well as our bishops have critically important gatekeeping responsibilities. The well-being of the church will be determined by how well that task is done. This is why many United Methodists have a continuing concern about United Methodist bishops who demonstrated at the 2000 General Conference in disagreement with their church's (and the Scripture's) teachings about homosexuality. This is why many are deeply distressed when a United Methodist bishop denies publicly and without apology the classic understandings of Jesus' full and unique deity, his virgin birth, blood atonement, and bodily resurrection—and does so while lecturing authoritatively to future ministers studying at one of our United Methodist seminaries.

I remember reading words from Catholic Cardinal Joseph Ratzinger a few years ago, when he was speaking to American Archbishops prior to becoming Pope. He lamented the fact that many of his church's theologians and academicians had adopted the relativism of the present day. Sadly, he noted, the bishops are failing to challenge them and are not confronting them with the authority of the truth. Ratzinger then made this memorable comment: "It's the hallmark of truth to be worth suffering for." (Leaving room, he allowed, for intellectual debate.) He went on to say that the faithful have a right to know which theologians are right and which wrong. "This kind of authoritative teaching," he insisted, "is the job of bishops—even at the cost of popularity, even at the cost of martyrdom."

November/December 2002

THIRTY-FOUR

Time for change at the Women's Divison

We have voiced concerns previously about the Women's Division's policies and resources. Specifically, we have been concerned for years about radical feminist, pro-abortion, virulently anti-American, anti-evangelical, anti-free market, and pro-homosexual attitudes exhibited by the Division's New York leadership and materials.

The United Methodist Women have a wonderful history and heritage in American Methodism. One can't imagine all that is done in local church ministry, including the furtherance of world mission outreach, without thinking about the remarkable contribution across the years of the United Methodist Women.

But something has gone very wrong with the Women's Division in New York. The actions taken at the Division's meeting last fall (2001) served only as a catalyst for Good News' call for reform of the Women's Division—its leadership, policies, and emphases. These problems did not appear just recently. We have been concerned about them for years.

What problems? To put it succinctly, the Women's Division has become a very wealthy and powerful agency with enormous influence in voting strength and funding. The $20 million it provides annually to mission via the General Board of Global Ministries, along with its investment income, make it the most powerful influence on that giant board. The problem, it seems to us, is that the Women's Division operates with *no accountability* to the rest of the church. This was seen clearly in December of 2000 when the Women's Division closed its National Gathering of Teens and College/University Women (*Young*

Woman, Rise Up!) to all press reporters or observers, *even* the United Methodist News Service! This was done despite protests from United Methodist news outlets. The Division felt free to violate the "open meeting" policy of the *Discipline* and thumb its nose at the entire church.

We have voiced concerns previously about the Women's Division's policies and resources. Specifically, we have been concerned for years about radical feminist, pro-abortion, virulently anti-American, anti-evangelical, anti-free market, and pro-homosexual attitudes exhibited by the Division's New York leadership and materials. That, I realize, is a serious charge. One should not make such claims without considerable collaborative evidence. Nor should one believe such a charge without checking out that evidence.

As a part of our Call to Reform, our RENEW Network President, Faye Short, has produced a White Paper entitled "Our Basis For Concern." It is a 14-page, impeccably-documented account of questionable actions and positions of the Women's Division during the last three decades. Good News and RENEW, our women's program arm, are fully aware that we alone cannot bring reform to the Women's Division. If it happens, it must come from United Methodist women themselves, as well as from UM pastors, who are *ex officio* members of the local unit and of its executive committee (*Discipline*, Par. 255.4, Article 4).

I urge all who read this to get our White Paper and read about these concerns. It is a sobering chronicle. You will discover, for example:

• In 1973, the Women's Division helped start the (pro-abortion) Religious Coalition for Abortion Rights, now called the Religious Coalition for Reproductive Choice (RCRC), and the Women's Division is listed on their letterhead to this day. Also, in April, 1996, the Women's Division endorsed a letter sent to U.S. House of Representative members by RCRC expressing agreement with President Clinton's veto of the "Partial-Birth Abortion Ban," a bill which had strong bi-partisan support from both houses of Congress.

• In Deputy General Secretary Joyce Sohl's report to the Women's Division, April 12, 1991, she cited a definition of a "multicultural community" as one which "stresses an appreciation for the impact of differences—race, class, age, sex, physical, sexual/affectional orientation, and religious." She added, "I have a vision of the Women's Division being a multicultural community where the contribution of each is valued." The reference to sexual/affectional orientation is clear. Furthermore, the Women's Division has invited Ms. Barbara Lundblad to speak at the UMW Assembly this April. Looking at her messages at the '93 and '98 Re-Imagining Conferences, Faye Short notes that Ms. Lundblad was a strong proponent of radical feminist theology, advocated for the acceptance of homosexual/lesbian practice, and referred to Jesus as the "child of Sophia."

• In the 1992/93 mission study *We Belong Together*, Rosemary Radford Reuther's book *Women-Church* was lifted up as a favorable guide for women. A close look at the ceremonies and rituals in Reuther's book, including the ritual for a same-sex union, shows them to be neo-pagan, woefully lacking in sound Christian theology.

These are just brief samplings. As you read the entire White Paper, I believe you will agree it is past time for a thorough reassessment, re-evaluation, and reform of the Women's Division.

March/April 2002

THIRTY-FIVE

The Bishops' Pastoral misses the mark

Augustine, Aquinas, Luther, and others have believed that Christians could and should join in exercising civil authority. To do so was to fulfill the church's teaching that government is instituted by God to punish the wrongdoer, reward and protect the good, and preserve peace.

The United Methodist Council of Bishops concluded its fall meeting by issuing a pastoral letter in response to the terrorist attacks of September 11 and the war against terrorism.

A quick read of the pastoral letter might see it as just a brief, measured statement with several concerns and directives for how we should pray. However, a more careful reading leaves one disappointed, both at what it said and at what it *didn't* say. And learning what got cut from the original draft only adds to one's distress.

Around the same time, a pastoral message was issued by the U.S. Conference of Catholic Bishops. There is a striking contrast between the two in terms of theological and intellectual substance. The United Methodist pastoral is woefully weak in comparison to the thoughtful, substantive statement of the United States Catholic Bishops. One wonders if our UM bishops have not somehow lost touch with more than a millennium of church teaching, having become disconnected from what Richard Neuhaus calls "the Great Tradition of Christian thought."

In terms of things *said*, the bishops' pastoral makes the stunning claim that "violence in all its forms and expressions is contrary to God's purpose for the world." One blinks with astonishment at this claim! Were this to be true, there would be no place for a nation's armed forces or for that matter, a community's police force. Swiss theologian Emil Brunner has written, "To deny on ethical grounds the elementary right of the state to defend itself by war simply means to deny the existence of the state itself. Pacifism of the absolutist variety is practical anarchy."

The original draft of the letter, aptly prepared by Bishop Joe Pennel of Virginia, condemned terrorism by saying, "Terrorism in all its forms and expressions is contrary to God's dream for the world." That would have been a welcomed statement. However, Bishop Joe Sprague of Northern Illinois suggested the phrase be changed from "terrorism" to "violence" and changed the statement to: "violence in all of its forms and expressions is contrary to God's purpose for the world." Unfortunately, the suggested change by Bishop Sprague, a pacifist, drastically altered the meaning of the entire pastoral letter. I am surprised that other bishops didn't protest this egregious change.

This statement from the UM bishops was released two days before Veterans Day—a day set aside to honor and thank the men and women who valiantly put their lives in the line of fire to ensure our freedoms in this country. Can you imagine reading the statement from the UM bishops to a group of World War II veterans? Their chief pastors would have been saying to them that what they did to end Nazism was "contrary to God's purpose for the world."

Then, there are important things not said in the UM pastoral. The original draft cited the Social Principles from *The Book of Discipline*, which acknowledge that "most Christians regretfully realize that, when peaceful alternatives have failed, the force of arms may be preferable to unchecked aggression, tyranny, and genocide" (Par. 164. G). Unfortunately, this was cut from the final draft. The original also referred to the horrific events of September 11 as a "shattering evil." The final letter made no mention of "evil." Though several bishops asked that prayers for the U.S. military be included, the final draft makes no reference to our armed forces (except chaplains), requesting prayer rather for people "placed in harm's way and their loved ones." Our bishops seemed unwilling to ask prayer specifically for "the U.S. armed forces."

Sadly, there was little passion or sense of outrage in our bishops' letter. The Catholic bishops' message, by contrast, is not dispassionate. It refers to "those who committed these atrocities" (and that is what the events of September 11 were—atrocities, not merely "sad and terrible events" as the UM bishops say). The Catholic leaders insist, "The dreadful deeds of September 11 cannot go unanswered." And again, "We acknowledge...the right and duty of a nation and the international community to use military force if necessary to defend the common good..." They add that this must be done according to sound moral principles, the norms of the just war tradition.

For centuries, the Christian Church has taught that the governing authority is "the servant of God to execute wrath on the wrongdoer" (Romans 13:5). Augustine, Aquinas, Luther, and others have believed that Christians *could* and *should* join in exercising civil authority. To do so was to fulfill the church's teaching that government is instituted by God to punish the wrongdoer, reward and protect the good, and preserve peace.

In this important teaching, Richard Neuhaus notes that just war "is not itself an evil; nor is it even, as is commonly said today, a necessary evil. It is, if just, a positive duty, the doing of which, while it may entail much suffering, is to be counted as a good."

The omission of any reference to just war in the bishops' pastoral, at this time in our nation's history, is a serious, even embarrassing, omission.

January/February 2002

THIRTY-SIX

Conduct worthy of the gospel

Others have left because of the conference leadership's persistent neglect of church law and doctrine. With 67 clergy participating in a same-sex union, a conference Committee on Investigation dropping charges, and a bishop applauding it all, you have a conference whose leadership is in rebellion against church law and discipline.

The tragic turmoil that continues to unfold in the California/ Nevada Annual Conference is a scene without precedence within United Methodism. Let me review briefly what has happened there. (For a fuller account, see Good News, September/October 2000.)

In 1998, five evangelical pastors left the conference to minister outside the United Methodist Church. Those leaving included the Revs. Ed Ezaki, Kevin Clancey, John Christie, Rich Harrell, and Andy Vom Steeg. (I want you to see their names and realize they are real pastors with families, children, and congregations who loved them.)

They were leaders in the conference's Evangelical Renewal Fellowship (ERF), a group of evangelical clergy and laity whose disenchantment with conference policies and marginalization of evangelicals had led them to petition the 2000 General Conference for status as an Evangelical Missionary Conference. (Their request was denied by a 615-312 vote, which showed considerable support for the request.)

In 1999, the Rev. Don Fado and 68 clergy co-officiants from the conference blessed a same-sex union of lay leaders Ellie Charlton and Jeanne Barnett. Charges were brought against the clergy, but a Committee on Investigation in the conference voted not to press charges. Bishop Melvin Talbert, now retired, publicly defended the action, saying, "There is another more basic and fundamental covenant" than the *Book of Discipline*.

The Judicial Council overruled Talbert's claim last May in Cleveland, stating that "a clergy person [and bishop] has the responsibility of adhering to the provisions of the *Discipline* and to assure that those for whom he/she has administrative responsibility do the same." Not to do so, the ruling added, "would lead to chaos in the Church." Chaos, we would note, is what we now see in this annual conference.

Then, in March of this year, six evangelical pastors issued an open letter to the conference saying their church's apportionment payments would be redirected to an escrow account in protest of the rebellion of their annual conference leadership. Bishop Talbert responded by filing formal complaints against the six. The result: since June, eight more pastors have left the denomination to minister elsewhere. This includes the Revs. Kyle Phillips, John Motz, Greg Smith, John Sheppard, Peter Kraemer, Ray O'Neil, Ben Kelley, and Luiz Lemos. (Again, you need to see their names.)

So, to date, 13 pastors have terminated their relationship with the California/Nevada Annual Conference. All were gifted, effective evangelicals serving vital, growing churches. These are the kind of pastors we cannot afford to lose.

Paul urged the Christians at Philippi, "Whatever happens, conduct yourselves in a manner worthy of the gospel of Christ" (Philippians 1:27). We must ask whether the actions of this conference's leadership is conduct "worthy of the gospel of Christ?" Why such turmoil? Why have these pastors left?

Some who have left speak about the oppression they have felt and the hostility they have experienced from their conference leadership; they speak of their bishop who, when asked why he had no evangelicals on his cabinet, replied, "Look, I need to appoint people whom I can trust implicitly, because they represent me." (That will qualify as the most *exclusive* statement of the decade.) Evangelicals in the conference have felt disenfranchised for years.

Others have left because of the conference leadership's persistent neglect of church law and doctrine. With 67 clergy participating in the blessing of a same-sex union, a conference Committee on Investigation dropping charges, and a bishop applauding it all, you have a conference whose leadership is in rebellion against church law and discipline.

In addition, pastors have left because of serious violations of due process. The Revs. Kyle Phillips and Luiz Lemos were called in this spring by Bishop Talbert and reprimanded—Phillips for "arrogance and condescension" and Lemos for supposedly "alienating a significant number of people." Both were told they would be moving (both to much smaller congregations and Lemos after just ten months at his current appointment). Neither were allowed an advocate and neither's Pastor-Parish Relations Committee was consulted. Both moves were purely punitive; they were exercises of raw episcopal power. Both seriously violated due process according to the *Book of Discipline*. Sadly, Phillips and Lemos are now gone.

The California/Nevada Annual Conference clearly has been marching to its own drumbeat. The result, as predicted by the Judicial Council, is "chaos in the Church." Some liberal conferences seem to view evangelicals more like a white supremacist cult than as brothers and sisters in Christ. In a report to his annual conference this spring, one prominent liberal pastor referred to evangelicals as "slime," with no challenge from the presiding bishop. Friends, something is seriously wrong. This is not conduct "worthy of the gospel of Christ."

Let's pray earnestly that new episcopal leadership might, at a minimum, bring a new attitude of justice and respect in the California/Nevada Annual Conference.

November/December 2000

THIRTY-SEVEN

When a bishop breaks a covenant

*More recently, a pastor was tried for performing
a same-sex covenant, and was acquitted.
On the day the verdict was announced,
92 pastors (now more than 200), pledged they
will perform (or continue performing) same-sex
covenants, and nothing has been said about them.*

In 1996, Abingdon Press released Lyle E. Schaller's 40th book, *Tattered Trust*. Some readers acclaimed it as his best. In the book, Schaller examines the waning trust of local congregations toward their denomination with a seasoned, sometimes painful analysis.

If trust had become "tattered" in 1996 within United Methodism, it may now be shredded.

The swirling controversy over the acquittal of the Rev. Jimmy Creech, the Omaha pastor tried for performing a same-sex covenant, forced United Methodist bishops to take time during their April (1998) meeting to issue a Pastoral Letter to the Church. The letter affirmed their commitment "to uphold the General Conference's action on the theological, ethical, and polity matters defined in the *Book of Discipline*, including statements on homosexuality and all specified issues contained in the Social Principles including the prohibition of ceremonies celebrating homosexual unions by our ministers and in our churches." The two-page statement was approved unanimously and was widely heralded across the church.

However, *within just two weeks* of the release of the bishops' pastoral, the trust level felt by congregations toward the Council of Bishops, already "tattered," took another heavy blow. Bishop Melvin G. Talbert, (California/Pacific Annual Conference) sent a letter to the clergy and lay members of his conference saying he does not consider a pastor's performing a "holy union" (same-sex covenant) to be a violation of church law.

In his letter, Talbert acknowledged that performing such a same-sex union "does go against the spirit" of the United Methodist Social Principles—where it is specifically forbidden. But the Social Principles "are not law," he said. This was written, I would remind you, less than two weeks after Bishop Talbert joined in the unanimous vote of the Council stating that they would uphold the standards in the *Book of Discipline* "including statements on homosexuality" and specifically *"including the prohibition of ceremonies celebrating homosexual unions by our ministers and in our churches"* (emphasis mine).

Such a casual dismissal of the Pastoral Letter—a covenant actually—that Bishop Talbert had shared with his other episcopal colleagues, leaves many United Methodists with a profound sense of betrayal. Others on the Council of Bishops may feel that as well.

It was these actions, in addition to the actions of churches in his area, all publicly known and documented, that led the Good News executive committee to call upon Bishop Talbert to resign from his episcopal office, as an act of personal integrity, and take early retirement. Obviously, the bishop is unwilling to "live in covenant with one another," nor is he willing to uphold the church's standards on homosexuality. As a matter of principle, he should resign. The Council of Bishops, which spoke much of corporate accountability in Lincoln, should now exercise it.

Why is United Methodist trust so "tattered" and shredded? Consider the history of struggle over this one issue. We first passed the "incompatibility" statement about homosexual practice in 1972. In 1984, after learning what we had in the *Book of Discipline* was not binding, General Conference passed the statement prohibiting the ordination and appointment of "self-avowed practicing homosexuals." It *was* binding. Soon, folks charged we had not defined "self-avowed practicing," and it was determined that conference Boards of Ordained Ministry would have to develop their own working definitions. Then the Oregon/Idaho Conference Clergy approved for elder's orders a candidate its Board of Ministry acknowledged to be a "self-avowed practicing homosexual." She was subsequently appointed.

Then, in 1996, 15 bishops stunned General Conference (and the church) by releasing a public statement about their "pain" over the church's standards on homosexuality. Despite the bishops' public statement, the delegates in Denver passed the statement prohibiting same-sex covenants being performed by our ministers or conducted in United Methodist churches. It was challenged because of its placement in the *Book of Discipline*. More recently, a pastor was tried for performing a same-sex covenant, and was acquitted. On the day the verdict was announced, 92 pastors pledged they would perform (or continue performing) same-sex covenants, and nothing has been said about them. [Today, the number of pastors who have pledged is over 200.] The Council of Bishops, sensing a crisis in the church, released a pastoral letter promising to uphold the church's standards—a letter supposedly passed unanimously. In less than two weeks, the letter was publicly ignored by one of the bishops and his cabinet.

No wonder there's a crisis of trust within the United Methodist Church on the part of the laity toward their leaders. When churches withhold, redirect, or just stop giving funds, our bishops should not blame the "crisis talk." They must give the church faithful and courageous leadership on this issue—a very divisive controversy that has been tearing at the unity and vitality of our church for more than 25 years. The United Methodist Church desperately needs faithful episcopal leadership.

July/August 1998

Acknowledgments:

Once again, I want to thank my colleagues at Good News who have helped me time and again across the years be a better writer than I am. I am especially grateful to Steve Beard and numerous editorial assistants for their counsel, ideas, suggestions, and careful editing in my regular writing responsibilities here at Good News. Their professionalism and expertise have left me in their debt.